Woodland Plants and Sun-lovers

by the same authors

MAKING A SHRUB GARDEN

Woodland Plants
and Sun-lovers

HAROLD and JOAN
BAWDEN

THE GARDEN BOOK CLUB
121 Charing Cross Road London WC2

First published in 1970
by Faber and Faber Limited
24 Russell Square London WC1
Printed in Great Britain by
Latimer Trend & Co Ltd Plymouth
All rights reserved

This edition by arrangement with
Faber and Faber Limited 1971

CONTENTS

Foreword by Will Ingwersen   *page* 11

Preface   13

Introduction   15

1. Some Sun-Lovers and Exotics   19

2. Favourite Herbaceous Perennials   39

3. A Few Front-line Perennials   54

4. The Evergreen Woodlanders   70

5. Other Plants for Shade and Part Shade   86

6. Architectural Plants   109

7. Silver and Grey, Variegated Foliage and Grasses   122

8. Carpeters, Ground-cover and Weed Suppressors   133

9. Odds and Ends, and Gentians   148

   Index   173

ILLUSTRATIONS

between pages 32 and 33

Eucomis comosa
Eucomis comosa
Dimorphotheca ecklonis 'Prostrata'
Schizostylis 'Mrs Heggarty'
Hemerocallis double variety
Iris tectorum
Dimorphotheca barberiae
Anemone tetrasepala
Thermopsis montana
Lychnis dioica flore pleno
Oenothera glaber

between pages 80 and 81

Woodland scene
Galax aphylla
Astrantia major
Arum creticum
Boykinia aconitifolia
Roscoea humeana
Erythroniums
Lysimachia ciliata
Erythronium 'White Beauty'
Melittis melissophyllum

ILLUSTRATIONS

between pages 112 and 113

Tricyrtis macropoda
Digitalis ferruginea
Sisyrinchium striatum
Rogersia
Euphorbia mellifera
Phormium tenax
Iris pallida 'Variegata'
Helichrysum fontanesii
Hieracium bombycinum
Miscanthus sinensis 'Variegatus'

between pages 144 and 145

Geranium grevilleanum
Iris innominata aurea
Cornus canadensis
Campanula jenkinsae
Gentiana × *macaulayi*
Gentiana pneumonanthe
Zigadenus elegans
Gentiana makinoi
Delphinium brunonianum
Polemonium pauciflorum

FOREWORD

BOOKS ABOUT gardening roll off the presses in a never ending stream and are eagerly read by an ever increasing number of garden and plant lovers. I read most of them, as I did Harold and Joan Bawden's first book. I much enjoyed the simply told narrative in which they described *Making a Shrub Garden*.

This foretaste of their ability to write a delightfully readable book about the plants which mean so much to them added to the pleasure given to me by their invitation to write a foreword to their second book.

I am sure that *Woodland Plants and Sun-lovers* will give those who read it in its completed form as much pleasure as it has given me to read it in manuscript. It is not a learned book, but Harold and Joan Bawden's great love for plants is made abundantly clear on every page of a book which will be enjoyed by novice and expert alike. It contains a wealth of information for those who, like these knowledgeable authors, set out to make a garden.

Their beautiful garden on the edge of Ashdown Forest, in the rolling Sussex Weald, is well known to me and I have spent many hours of delight in the sanctuary which these two ardent gardeners literally carved out of a wild hillside.

WILL INGWERSEN, V.M.H.

PREFACE

IN OUR previous book we wrote about garden making and our shrubs, but they are only part of a garden, the majority of them flowering earlier in the year. One cannot have too many shrubs in the small garden, or there is lack of colour in the later months. The answer to this is the perennial plants that maintain the interest and give a display right into the late autumn. We feel that with so many new gardens and garden owners the wide interest and popularity of plants and flowers is nowhere near its peak. We have been asked by so many people what plants they can grow in shady places, that we have included many plants that will be quite happy in the smallest of gardens.

Besides many ordinary perennials which will always be indispensable, our aim has also been to bring to notice many of the more interesting and uncommon ones that new gardeners will want to know about.

As regards the naming of plants, there are so many anomalies that it can be puzzling even to the experts. We cannot claim to be among the latter—we just love our plants. Names are always changing, but we have used the familiar catalogue names as they have been, and may be found at present, but where there is a synonym the New R.H.S. Supplement is our authority and the name by which a plant is generally known follows in brackets. Thus we hope to satisfy the expert and help the reader who may be searching for plants. Much of the praise for this part must go to Mr. Will Ingwersen, V.M.H. and Miss Ann Bonar for their criticisms and suggestions and in helping to check the manuscript.

Some of the photographs are taken by ourselves and the

majority taken in the garden by another keen gardener Mr. John Davies. We must also express our thanks to Mr. Donald Merrett and to Mr. Roy Elliott for the use of their monochrome plates. Finally, we should like to thank Mrs. Sylvia Bassam for helping with the chore of typing, the least interesting part to us, for we find that typewriters do not always do what we want them to do!

Woodland Plants and Sun-lovers

INTRODUCTION

THIS IS AN account of plants that we grow in our own garden, an area which consists of part woodland, and sandy sunny slopes where sun-loving plants enjoy the elevation to the sun and the good drainage. The parts which have gradually grown up to form woodland and woodland conditions have also given us great pleasure, for here we have been able to grow many plants that do not usually succeed in the full sun of the open garden.

There is no doubt that woodland gardening has its own fascination; it is so natural in its composition and makes a happy and harmonious home for some of nature's most lovely plants. Not only is there the beauty of the trees and shrubs that help to form it, but it is the conditions of light and shade that have gradually evolved as it has grown up that have made it suitable for a greater variety of plants.

While the natural woodland is ideal, let none believe that some of the most beautiful woodland plants that are described cannot be grown in a small garden. In most gardens, and town ones too, there is some shade or degree of shade from walls or fences, from the house, or even neighbouring trees, which can be put to good account. There are few plants which need dense shade all the time, and the greater number succeed with light shade and the fleeting hours of sun that they are given in its passing circle. So many beautiful plants will thrive and be happy on the shady side of the house that quite a wide range of choice ones can be grown as long as the border is wide enough and there is sufficient moisture and good drainage.

Sometimes these house borders will face north or east, which will give ample sun in the morning. Likewise the western exposure will be partly shaded for most of the day, but will get ample light and sun in the latter end of the day. Quite the best of the woodland treasures can be accommodated in these borders and enjoyed throughout the year at one's doorstep without the necessity of tramping across squelching lawns. They can be full of interest all the year, first the snowdrops, then the cheery cyclamen in spring and autumn, the early erythroniums, the miniature astilbes for the later summer, and so much more to fill in between. These places may call for the compact growers and those of dependable height, erect and non-invasive. Such plants as hepaticas, *Cardamine trifolia*, *Astilbe glaberrima* 'Saxatilis', the miniature London Prides, *Saxifraga fortunei*, *Iris gracilipes*, the synthyris and many others mentioned in the shade chapters, are among those which will be slow growing and compact. For a touch of glorious winter colour the shortias and schizocodons can scarcely be bettered, while such plants as *Anemonopsis macrophylla*, *Tiarella trifoliata*, the francoas, dentarias and roscoeas give their qualities of fairy grace and exotic flower, and then the podophyllums and various other foliage plants add a handsomeness of leaf.

If we were planning a woodland in a small garden, we would visualise a few trees or tall shrubs to be seen from the house, a vista that would include a few conifers of yellow or gold for winter effect. There would be flowering trees of beauty such as the Japanese cherries, and the pyrus and sorbus for their autumn fruits. These would give height and create a small woodland, give protection from hot sun and provide light shade or dappled shade. Without listing too many, we would include viburnums, then hamamelis and acers for their beauty of form and autumn colour. A few azaleas, evergreen and deciduous, would be very effective as lower shrubs for ground-cover.

In this imaginary garden the placing of the larger trees would be fairly wide so that space would be ample without planting too near the roots of the trees which can rob the soil of moisture. The soil should be well prepared by a good spade's depth digging and an abundance of peat or leaf-soil dug into it. If this were a town garden, we imagine the wilder part emerging from the formal garden through as wide a grass path as space will allow, to form a glade between the trees. Even in the smallest of gardens a few of the taller cotoneasters or philadelphus, placed well away from the sides of the path, can create the effect of a glade. The result of walking back from the wild and less tamed part of the garden into the formal and tamed part is a great contrast and can be compared to walking back into civilization—two worlds in a small space!

On a hot day we walk back from our woodland into the sunshine and a different temperature, where the sun-lovers are enjoying every moment of it, maturing and even preparing for the next year's display. Yet, there are between-stages before we come to more open beds that the sun-lovers enjoy. We then come to medium and lower growing shrubs which let in more light to herbaceous plants which like to get their heads in the sun but have coolness at the root. Numbers of these are happy between the shrubs, and thus some of them have a natural setting and at the same time help to break up a tendency to a monotonous line of shrubs. This arrangement gives a certain amount of shelter, degrees of shade and lets in enough sun for the well being of the lower-growing plants.

Amongst the shrubs too, and in the foreground are the 'ground-cover plants' and 'weed suppressors'. These do a good job for us, carpeting what might be empty spaces or room for weeds, and also conserving moisture in the soil. The majority of these are low-growing plants, ones which are easily stepped over to get at taller plants or shrubs. Their likes and dislikes are fully dealt with in the chapter on ground-cover plants (Chapter 9) as well as those which are very suitable for the paved garden.

While the ground-cover plants form their worth-while and colourful carpet for the scene, the front-line perennials, as we have chosen them, are low-growing plants for any sunny border. The majority of them are for easy gardening, plants that can be left to their own devices, require no staking and will provide a good backbone for a midget border, the kind of plants that are useful in approach borders to the house.

The architectural plants are important for contrast, to make an arresting and bold feature at a focal point or for their nobleness of stature. Even the midget border can have its architectural plant for contrast as long as it is not too large and out of character with the smaller plants.

Then there are the silver- and grey-foliaged plants and grasses, so necessary to give distinction and relieve a surplus of colour. The grasses can be very impressive as specimens and give a great variety of soft shades. They provide graceful flowering plumes and are as important as the architectural plants. The silver- and grey-foliaged plants and the glaucous-leaved ones give original and picturesque contrast and add an uncommon touch to the most ordinary border. They help to relieve and break up any uniformity of green and, where there is high colour, such as shades of red or crimson, a background or underplanting of grey or silver will accentuate the picture. Though we are no advocates of bedding out, an example would be the silvery-grey foliage of *Centaurea gymnocarpa* used as such an effective foil to the spectacular colours of the cannas in the beds at Wisley. The more silvery-whiteness of the leaf, the more impressive is the result. Two such outstanding plants are *Senecio cineraria* and its cultivar *S*. 'White Diamond', which light up a space of ground with their mass of serrated foliage throughout the year. Then there are the lighter touches that some of the artemisias provide, a beauty of leaf in feathery, delicately cut foliage. Perhaps the most artistic results come from the use of grey and silver with the softer shades—blending more in harmony! Then there are the taller plants such as *Perowskia atriplicifolia* with its tapering greyish stems, as well as the spectacular *Verbascum bombyciferum* with the silvery-woolliness of Father Christmas, or the onopordons in lofty silvery-white.

Like all books, this is not a complete list of plants, but we have tried to classify them and show their requirements in the south of England, and as we have it, on a light sandy, acid soil. Inevitably they overlap, the half-shady plants and the ground-covering ones and some of the front-line perennials.

In spite of our love for our shrubs which are described in our book *Making a Shrub Garden*, it is undeniable that for colour, many of these perennials have the final say in the mid-summer days when the majority of the shrubs have finished. Thus we intermingle many of these ground-cover plants and other perennials which are described, so that they blend to make a harmonious whole to prolong our season of colour. The following chapters are a record of some of our perennial plants, ones which we have now, and some that we have grown in other gardens.

❊ I ❊

Some Sun-lovers and Exotics

FOR THE sun-loving plants it is best to choose the very open spaces, unshaded by any trees and if possible fully exposed to the sun at all times. The most favourable places are near sunny walls where plants, which are often too tender for the open garden, can be hardy and flower freely. If your garden has a gentle slope so much the better, for the drainage will be good. Those who have a level site need not be deterred, for if one aims at perfection, this could be made equally good by raising it with extra soil. If the soil is heavy, plenty of grit, weathered ashes and peat will help to lighten it and improve the drainage.

Much of our own soil is somewhat lean, hungry and sandy and many of these sun-lovers thrive in it, but we have found that those that resent this thin diet can often be persuaded to do much better in our lower garden where the water table is a little higher, but at the same time where the soil has been raised a few inches to get the better drainage.

On the whole, the light sandy soil is the best medium for the sun-lovers and its texture can always be improved by the addition of compost, peat, leaf-soil or some hop manure. In places where our own was almost pure silver sand, the addition of heavier soil well mixed in, proved to be very successful. While light soil has its limitations owing to its lack of humus, it has many advantages, especially as it can be worked at almost any time. Practically all grey and silver foliage plants like it and revel on warm dry slopes and many of the bulbous plants prefer it. Plants may not make such hearty growth as in a fatter soil but they keep much more compact and very often flower all the more freely. The plants that

19

do well in it are many perennial sun-lovers from the Mediterranean, South Africa and other sunny mountain sides, those of
America and the Atlas mountains, all appreciating the fast
drainage and elevation to the sun.

From America we have the evening primroses, mostly desert
plants which relish the warm sand, and winter all the better for
this sharp drainage. Coming after the first flush of the summer
flowers, their great cupped flowers look mysterious in the evening
light, and in the dusk attract the flitting moths. *Oenothera missourensis* (syn. *O. macrocarpa*) is perhaps the best known of these, a
most satisfying plant that is long lived and seems almost indestructible, but this you will find lives amongst our front row
border plants.

The exotic, huge, evanescent cups of *O. acaulis* (syn. *O. taraxacifolia*) are even larger, the purest of white in the late evening and
into the early morning, a good time to see it as the early shadows
play upon it. Then by breakfast time they are fading to the palest
of pink—their day is over! Starting from a rosette of dandelion-
like foliage, its flowers can be expected in early July. From then
onwards it extends long, prostrate flowering arms out to some
2–3 feet, continuing to bloom into November. Hanging from the
top of a warm wall it is superb, but equally magnificent trailing
down sunny slopes. If sown in the spring, the resulting plants
will flower the following year.

The showy *O. odorata* 'Sulphurea' is biennial, but is always with
us from self-sown seedlings. It is an erect grower with a number
of slender 2–2½-foot stems and a long succession of 2½-inch-wide
fragrant yellow flowers from June onwards. Self-sown seedlings
should be moved when quite young, as they soon form a long tap
root. Another white one, though seemingly short lived, is *O.
trichocalyx*. In spite of this it can be treated as an annual, for it will
bloom seven to eight weeks from a March sowing. Here again is
a very beautiful pure white which not only blooms for a long
time, but whose flowers open in the morning. The blossoms are
almost as large as those of *O. acaulis* but the plant is semi-erect
growing with greyish-green leaves.

Another American plant of the plains, a member of the mallow
family which does well in this country, is *Callirhoe involucrata*. It is

a good perennial, an exotic and brilliant plant that nearly all visitors fall for. A prostrate grower, it sends out 2–3-foot-long flowering stems from a central rosette. The cluster of flowers are carried on the ends of the stems as they lengthen, and then they continue to extend and bloom from July right into the autumn. This gives a startling display of large, silky-sheeny, inch-wide cups of magenta or port wine colour which, falling downhill or over a wall, are a thrilling picture.

As a contrast to these low growers, *Moraea spathacea* of the iris family, makes a clump of long, dark, grassy evergreen leaves. In spite of coming from Cape Province and the Transvaal, this is perfectly hardy in full sun and well-drained soil, and we have seen it doing well enough in the warmer parts of a garden on stiff clay. It has bright yellow, iris-like flowers which stand up well above the foliage on strong 15–18-inch stems. A little smaller than the general run of iris flowers, and with a slight fragrance, there is a refinement about them which should earn the plants a place in more gardens. Contrary to the repetitive information in some catalogues, it does not flower in March, but adds its performance to the feast of May flowers.

It is always a source of surprise how well a lot of these South Africans will do in this country, putting up a very satisfactory performance in spite of so much less sunshine. The agapanthus are now well established favourites, particularly *Agapanthus campanulatus* (syn. *A. umbellatus mooreanus*), which is certainly perfectly hardy in the south of England. Generally recommended as needing soil not too poor and dry, our largest clump of this is on the driest of sunny banks! Though we have wondered if it should be given a better chance, and if one year it may not prosper so well, it goes on from strength to strength, each year producing more spikes of bloom. Its mass of fleshy roots looks as though they could do with some good feeding, yet plants in better soil do not flower so well. Their heads of soft, clear blue flowers are held on sturdy 2-foot stems, and are most welcome in the later summer. With a neat array of strap-shaped leaves, they are tidy plants that fit well into the formal garden, or narrow border round the house. The white form of this is very beautiful and should be snapped up when offered.

They do not appear above ground again until late April, and strangely enough we always find the white form very much later. Under the name of 'Headbourne Hybrids', some wonderful strains can now be obtained. These are more robust in appearance and have sturdy stems of over 3 feet, carrying great heads of flowers in varying shades, pale blues, violet-blues and darker ones.

The well-known *A. africanus*, which used to be *A. umbellatus* of conservatories and summer tub culture, is also very much hardier than has been supposed, and we know of gardens in the south where it is just covered over with sacking or straw for the winter time. Furthermore, another large plant, grown right against a south wall, has never been protected! It has most ornamental and handsome foliage and large heads of violet-blue.

Of the South African crinums, quite a few are hardy and all well worth growing, but we have only been able to obtain the well-known *Crinum powellii*, now well tried for hardiness. With a mass of thick fleshy roots which spread around its massive bulb, it certainly does need some sustenance and repays deep, well-prepared soil, full sun and annual topdressings of manure. *C. powellii* flowers in late August, its strong stems suddenly coming up from the side of the bulb and up through the leaves, to reach 3 feet when suited. The numerous funnel-shaped, lily-like trumpets, of some 5–6 inches long, are regal and superb in deep pink, or white in the form *album*. Plenty of space should be allowed for its mass of dropping leaves.

Also supreme among the bulbous South Africans are the nerines and amaryllis, and these take their place in full sunshine at the foot of a warm south wall. We have grown *Nerine bowdenii* for many years, finding it most good tempered and very hardy, even the flowers standing a good number of degrees of autumn frost. Like the amaryllis, the nerines suddenly shoot up an entirely leafless stem which at 18 inches bears an umbel of lovely rose-pink flowers in late August, and will often still be out in November. If required for indoor decoration, the spikes should be cut just as the flowers are coming out—they will then last very well.

There should be others in this family which may prove hardy in the south. The only other one to come to us has been *N. filifolia* which has been out in the open for many years, increasing and wintering well until the 1963 winter when our small colony was reduced by half. It is a smaller plant, with thin grassy leaves and pink flowers on 10–12-inch stems. This is now increasing quite quickly again and would make a very good edging plant for any sunny border. Both these nerines may be carefully divided in the spring time, though we have moved *bowdenii* about in clumps at all sorts of times. *Amaryllis belladonna* is a late flowerer, dallying till the middle of October to put forth its very large soft, rosy-pink, funnel-shaped flowers, peerless and majestic on their strong 2-foot stems. But we patiently wait for our own to do this, and what a joy it will be when they have fattened and built strength to do so!

Though we have a 7-foot wall of some 30 feet below the house, and a walled and paved garden below that, the accommodation for these sun-lovers is always at a premium. Some of the cistus and other shrublets take their place, but room is always wanted for other favourites and doubtful hardies. That wonderful trailer, *Convolvulus mauritanicus* always has to have space, sometimes for a year or so, or more if the winters are kind. Now with a plant established right in the wall, our optimism sees it living for years. In sunny, well-drained soil, it is a joy from June till October, extending a mass of slender growths for feet around, and giving a most generous display of florin-sized lavender-blue flowers unsurpassed in poise and elegance. It is not hardy without some amount of coddling even in normal winters, but fortunately it is easily struck from summer cuttings which may be wintered in frames or greenhouse, or plants may be lifted and potted into fairly deep pots for replanting in April or May. Covering an old plant with dry peat or ashes will often bring it through a not too severe winter. Even more beautiful is *C. althaeoides*, silvery-grey of foliage and with larger, satiny-pink, funnel-shaped flowers. To see these fully open, gently shimmering to a summer breeze, is a lovely picture, but it has one drawback in that it has the invasive habit that the family is notable for! It is happy in poor stony soil and should be confined to places where its running habit can be checked.

Though some of these exotics and tenderish plants may be a little trouble, the reward is great, for they have such a long period of flower. *Dimorphotheca ecklonis* is yet another, a tender sub-shrubby plant from the Transvaal which does survive the winter at times, but again is easily struck from cuttings. Young plants grow rapidly if the weather is warm, and will reach 12–18 inches high in a season. It has great charm, with entrancing wide open, white daisy flowers with a shiny, velvety centre of dark violet. Its freedom of flower is more than matched by a form which sends out completely prostrate, flowering growths and an endless succession of identical flowers. It is fairly hardy and we accord it the most favoured places in the sun, for it is a first-class plant flowering from May till October. We believe, that this is the plant that is now sold as *D. ecklonis* 'Prostrata' and understand that it appeared as a chance seedling at Wisley with two other hybrids which seem to be crosses between *D. ecklonis* and *D. barberiae*. These two hybrids are strong growers and very showy plants, more upright in growth than either parent. Also, they are even more free flowering, giving a continuous succession of flowers from late May till November. One has large solid white flowers with the dark zone of *ecklonis*, and the other very large, soft pink flowers, both with the larger leaf of *D. barberiae*. These are really more or less on trial and have not yet had the test of a really severe winter; they may not be as reliably hardy as *D. barberiae*, but are plants that are so worth while for their flowering show.

Dimorphotheca barberiae itself, a Basutolander, is a wonderful ground-covering plant for sunny borders and is perfectly hardy. It is desirable for its refreshing, pleasantly aromatic, evergreen foliage and its 2-inch-wide, pink daisy flowers which stand up on 4-inch stems. *D. barberiae* 'Compacta' would be our own choice for the small garden, it is much less wide spreading, and gets its points for freedom of flower, but it is not evergreen.

These large-flowered composites are gay performers and though we are not given to bedding out, now and then we raise a batch of gazanias for places around the house. While they are not generally hardy, in favoured and well drained places we have had them survive mild winters. Yet, they are so easily raised from seed, they may be treated as annuals and grown from seed each year. If they are sown as early as February or March in gentle heat or a cold greenhouse, then planted out in late May, they will make bonny flowering plants by July. Those who might have criticized the type plant, *Gazania splendens* as perhaps a glorified marigold with just a dark centre, can hardly fail to find some pleasure in their modern version with an array of creams, golden-yellows, white, red and dusky purples. Some have the characteristic black central zone of *G. splendens* and others will have clear self colours. Compared with the general run of half-hardy perennials, theirs is a far longer display, a continuous succession of flower well into October if they have not been touched by frost. Any extra good forms may be lifted and wintered under glass, or cuttings may be taken in early September; this is a good time for either method. Under glass they will often continue to flower as late as December.

In warm places we have also used the trailing *Verbena peruviana* (syn. *V. chamaedrifolia*) to fill gaps, a few plants covering square feet in a few months; its intense scarlet is always cheerful and it blooms until September. *V.* 'Lawrence Johnson', more compact, a cherry red, is also good for sunny places in the foreground. Neither have any pretensions to being hardy, but a stock is easily maintained under glass. *V. rigida* (syn. *V. venosa*) has often surprised us by its ability to live as a perennial, especially where it is warm and freely drained. Our affection for this little plant goes back to past days of raising plants for filling gaps and bedding out. Its great asset is in its late summer show when it gives a generous display right up to frosty days, with heads of rich violet-purple flowers on wiry 12-inch stems—a neat little plant. When old growth is cut away in the spring, it will break away from below.

Another unusual plant of the sun-lovers is *V. bonariensis* which shoots up rather thin, square stems of 3–4 feet, and bears heads and side-branch flowers of lavender-violet in July and for many weeks afterwards. It is in effect a magnified version of the dainty, foot-high *V. rigida*, usually grown as an annual, but very often surviving a number of winters. As a group, *V. bonariensis* is effective with almost any lower-growing plants, and though looking dangerously top heavy, its square stem is strong and it generally waves quite comfortably to most breezes. Individual plants are not long lived, but seedings crop up with unfailing regularity. It comes from Brazil and takes the name of *V. patagonica* in some catalogues, the latter a plant described by Clay in *The Present*

Day Rock Garden, as 'a hard cushion of small rosettes'. Seizing upon this as something that would be choice for the rock garden, we were sold more 'coals to Newcastle'.

I think most gardeners are pleased when visitors are excited, attracted or appreciative of a beautiful plant, it makes everything all so worth while. *Sphaeralcea munroana* is one of these pleasures with inch-wide flowers of an enchanting and unusual shade of soft orange-pink or salmon-pink. Unfortunately it is not very easy to obtain and does not seem to set seed in this country. Coming from the arid regions of North America, it likes a sunny slope and its crown kept dry in winter time; by growing it in this way we have had it surviving for a number of years before we have needed to replace it from late summer cuttings. The prominent, sunny, downward slope always calls for a decorative plant with a long flowering season, and this member of the mallow family performs with a vigour and an abundance of flower from its 3–4-foot-long, semi-prostrate growths.

Another rare treasure of this sun-loving family is *Malvastrum lateritium*, a clump-forming plant sending up growths of 10–12 inches, upon which are set 2-inch-wide flowers of bewitching apricot, in late July and August. At one time this precious plant was lifted and potted up for the winter, but once we had a few spare plants it has gone into a permanent position in full sun and poor soil. So far it has survived three winters.

To us the Kaffir Lilies (*Schizostylis*) always call for some thought; they like sunshine and moisture, and our sunny slopes usually become rather dry. An extra depth of soil, some compost and a bit of weathered clay from our lower garden, seem to work well enough—and what a reward they can give. We like their dainty gladiolus-like spikes of flower in autumn, *Schizostylis coccinea* in deep red and *S*. 'Mrs Hegarty' in pale satiny-pink. Now there are earlier flowering cultivars which are most welcome. While perfectly hardy and hearty growers, 6–8 degrees (F) of frost may mar the flowers. They are perfect for the house and, if cut when the first few flowers are out, the rest will unfold in turn. If they should disappoint by blooming less freely, it is usually when they have become rather crowded; division and fresh soil will give them new vigour.

The incarvilleas also like the soil with a little more meat in it, but we have found them to be more permanent, their big deep, searching carroty roots all the better for the good drainage. *Incarvillea delavayi* is the tallest growing of the species, with big rosy-purple trumpet flowers on sturdy 2–2½-foot stems in June and July. *I. brevipes* is much the same, flowering a little earlier, at 12–15 inches high. *I.* 'Bee's Pink' is pale pink, and dwarf. All of them are best when planted in a group, their exotic flowers and lush, rather tropical looking foliage giving them an air of distinction in any position. They die away in the early autumn and usually appear again in the late weeks of April. *I. olgae* is distinct, a half-shrubby, flopping and sprawling plant up to 2 feet, with bell-shaped flowers of pale pink in summer. We have not yet had it flowering freely, though making plenty of foliage—perhaps it does not like our soil. The ferny-foliaged *I. variabilis* is rarely seen, but is well worth growing for the great variety of colours in their attractive pink, rose, cream and other shaded trumpets. It is perennial, but rather doubtfully so in this country.

Catananche caerulea is an old-world plant which came with us from our old cottage garden. In a lighter soil and against a sunny wall, the only place where it seemed to fit in a different type of garden, it is doing even better. It has a quiet charm with its dainty papery, blue cornflower-like blossoms in summer on wiry stalks 2–3 feet high.

The garden self-sowns are a bounty that help to fill and cheer many an odd spot. Sometimes they appear in what seems to be an unsuitable place, but sometimes nature's choice is good, and a beautiful picture is often the result. Any seedlings should be moved when they are young, and in showery weather there will be little check to their growth. *Celsia cretica* is a plant which provides many seedlings, and its thin, verbascum-like spikes of flowers fit in almost anywhere. It is a newer plant, and forms an interesting, crinkly, dark-leaved rosette of evergreen leaves. Its flower spike starts its long succession of yellow flowers in June, continuing to lengthen up to 3 feet, blossoming all the time till late summer.

Yet another sun worshipper and which never seems to mind being starved in rock crevices is *Limonium mouretii* (syn. *Statice mouretii*). This was given to us years ago by an old gardening friend—another collector of plants. It is a very distinct statice with an interesting flat rosette of glaucous evergreen leaves. It flowers in August and September with attractive drooping spikes on which are heads of numerous white flowers encased in a papery brown sheath—the effect is unusual. Though it comes from Morocco, it seems to be content enough with our ration of sunshine; it is long lived and quite hardy.

For us the libertias function as ground-cover plants and fill-ups of especial interest because of their evergreen foliage. In spite of a persistent and recurring label of 'not hardy in all districts', we have always found them perfectly reliable in a variety of soils in the south of England—all survived unperturbed and flowered well after the 1963 winter. This was really a test, and to those who might hitherto have hesitated, don't, not only is their sword-like foliage ornamental, but a good green in winter time, and being closely packed it is a first-class weed suppressor. Though we always grow these in the fullest sun, a few spare clumps in the lower and colder parts of the garden flower with no less freedom. In all this is a small family, but those usually met with are *L. ixioides* and *grandiflora* which comes from New Zealand, and *L. formosa* from Chile. All bear 2–3-foot spikes of pure white flowers which last for many weeks from June onwards.

Three antirrhinum species deserve note as adoring dry slopes, as well as liking to be dry in winter time. In comparison to the old 'Snapdragons' that we used to take a delight in 'popping open' in our youth, the species are more lowly and demure, but have decided charm. *Antirrhinum asarina* (*Asarina procumbens*) from the Pyrenees is well established in many a garden, a trailing, scrambling plant that is very free flowering from June to August and even into November. Its big creamy flowers are thrust forward over large, soft, hairy, greyish leaves. It yields plenty of seed and its progeny like to find themselves a home in rocky crevices. The seed is very viable and we have known seedlings appear where an old plant had been grown many years before. Another one is *A. glutinosum* 'Roseum', a cliff-dweller from Spain. As long as this has a warm position or is planted in a wall where it gets perfect drainage, it is quite happy away from its southern home. It is an evergreen semi-shrubby bushlet of 6–8 inches, giving rosy snap-dragons from June onwards. Though surviving normal winters, it needs occasional renewing from cuttings.

To add to these, there is *A. sempervirens* which came to us quite by chance. It appeared beside a plant of *Dracocephalum hemsleyanum*, at a casual glance it seemed to be a child of the latter, but when the dracocephalum went to rest in the autumn, the seedling remained evergreen. After surviving the winter, it was duly moved and when it flowered it turned out to be *A. sempervirens*, a bushy little fellow of some 6 inches with sprays of small white flowers.

We have written of *Othonnopsis cheirifolia* as a sub-shrubby plant in our book about shrubs, but it is worthy of inclusion again. In any raised bed it is a favourite front-liner for its luscious, glaucous-blue foliage which spreads low and wide in sunny places. This June-flowering North African, in spite of its rather exotic, fleshy, cactus-like appearance, is quite hardy, but is not for low damp situations. Its broad-rayed orange daisies are very cheerful.

The salvias come among these sun lovers, for they have always intrigued us since we grew the Vatican sage *Salvia sclarea turkestanica* at home. The unique shapes of their helmeted flowers, those such as *sclarea* with its big pink bracts, their superbly brilliant and also muted shades, and fragrant foliage, all add to their fascination. With the exception of gardens of botanical interest, it is surprising how few of the species are seen when one considers their ease of cultivation. When we read that their homelands are Spain, Morocco, Mexico, Chile and other places that we might perhaps like to be in ourselves to avoid our winters, it is not surprising that some are not too hardy. It is equally a wonder how a good many of them survive and respond to the return of warmer days. Given an ordinary well-drained soil and warm sunny position, the majority are easily grown. Also, being very easily raised from seed, it is up to those who are adventurous to try a few of the more exciting ones.

Our meadow sage, *S. pratensis* which occurs in a number of countries, is well worth its place in a collection. This has dark to mid-blue helmets on 1–1½-foot stems, and is a useful little plant in the foreground. If the form *S. pratensis tenorii* can be obtained, it is outstanding with larger and deeper blue flowers; to be effective both of these should be planted in groups. Both flower from June to August.

Salvia haematodes and *S. nemorosa* 'Superba' (syn. *S. virgata* 'Nemorosa') are perhaps two of the best known border plants, the former well deserving its Award of Merit. In good soil *S. haematodes* will reach 3 feet, a wonderful mixer in the border or with roses, for its pale lavender-blue flowers tone well with almost all comers. For making a fine patch of darker colour the 18–24-inch *S. nemorosa* 'Superba' is one of the best. The effect of its massed spikes of violet-purple flowers is very striking and, with a long flowering time from July to August, there are many border plants of lighter foliage and colour which blend with it. It looks particularly good with *Phlox* 'Norah Leigh'.

The Vatican sage, *S. sclarea turkestanica*, though taller than our usual run of plants, grows in what we call our 'sand bed'. This is a large oval border of some 25–30 feet long which at one time was largely populated by very old plants of *Calluna vulgaris*. The soil is poor and sandy, but after a few years of digging in grass mowings, bracken and manure, is gradually becoming more fertile. A few plants of the Vatican sage were put in as 'fill ups' while we waited for a few rose species, cistus and other shrubs to get established. Though not at its splendid best, which can sometimes be almost 4 feet, at least it is happy enough to reproduce itself. The bluish-white flowers are surrounded by rosy-lavender bracts, giving a fine effect over a very long period—June to August. It is a biennial and should be sown early in the year, so that it has plenty of time to become really thriving and strong for flowering the next year.

Another rewarding one is *S. candelabrum* with branching heads of beautiful violet flowers with attractive white keels. It grows up to 3½–4 feet, and although we lost it in a hard winter, we shall certainly try again. An interesting and unusual sage which was brought to us from Yugoslavia is *S. glutinosa*, a very hardy one with yellow flowers. This is a strong grower, most suitable for the wilder parts of a garden, though in our sand bed its activities are somewhat curbed. With large, dark hairy leaves, it makes quite a handsome ground-cover plant, growing up to 2–3 feet and sprawling outwards. Like most of the sages its flowers are borne over a long period, June seeing its first whorls of large pale yellow flowers, and from then into September.

Salvia jurisicii is quite hardy, and lived for a number of years; we may not have seen it at its best and suspect that it died of starvation before we really knew our soil and its limitations in certain areas. With curiously cut foliage, it sends out low flowering growths and dark violet-blue flowers. Another time we would place it, with yellow-foliaged plants, such as *Veronica teucrium* 'Trehane' or *Lamium maculatum* 'Aureum'.

One of the most exciting of these sages is *S. involucrata* 'Bethellii', alas, only hardy in the most favoured districts. It is rather a late starter and does not begin to flower until August, but if the weather be kindly it will go on until October. On almost shrubby stems up to 3 feet, its large, hooded, carmine-rose blossoms are a magnificent sight, flowering at the top and on side branches. We always give this the most favoured of positions in the sunshine. We have wintered it outside by covering it with ashes, but unless it is a warm summer it does not grow fast enough to flower very much before frosts come. Usually we overwinter it in a frost-free greenhouse where it goes on blooming until December. It is very easily struck from cuttings which grow rapidly when put out in May.

The Mexican species, *S. fulgens*, is very startling but tender like the former and well worth any extra trouble for those who can give it the benefit of a warm wall. This also flowers late in the summer, and is at its best by September, giving flowers of a superb brilliant velvety scarlet from the top of its 3-foot spike and from all the side branches. At one time we had *S. chamaedryoides* for a few years, but have not been able to replace it. This grew on a warm rock garden ledge, a charming prostrate, trailing plant with clear blue flowers.

Carlina acaulis, the Alpine thistle, by reason of coming from the Alps, generally finds its home in the rock garden, but its decorative value earns it a place on dry sunny slopes in company with a mixture of other sun-lovers. When it has arisen from its winter rest it displays a handsome flat rosette of silvery-green, prickly leaves some 6 inches long. From this the flower stems rise a few inches to bear flat heads of shining silvery thistles over 2 inches across; these gradually turn light brown and last a considerable time. It is easily grown and needs poor soil to keep its compact character.

In comparison to the latter, *Dierama pulcherrimum* is a giant, but arising from any low planting it can be singularly picturesque as a specimen. This is another South African, but a very hardy perennial which can be valuable for its 18-inch iris-like foliage, and for the elegance of its graceful flowering wands which have earned it the name of Angel's Fishing-rods and Wandflower. These rise up to 4–5 feet or even more, but mercifully they are so flexible as to be completely storm- and wind-proof, swinging airily in complete abandon. The numerous pendulous bells droop gracefully from the flower stems in a long succession from July till August. Generally these are bright purple to claret shades, but by careful selection, the colour range now extends from pale pink to deep wine red. It is a bulbous plant which does best in good deep soil, well drained and in full sun. It dislikes disturbance and may lose its leaves after planting, but once new leaves are formed it is permanently evergreen; after moving it may take a year or so to give of its best. Now we have a new strain of dwarf hybrids which carry 'fishing-rods' of 2–3 feet, which make it very suitable for miniature borders and intimate planting spaces.

An old timer, and one that is often seen in old gardens, and which has been in cultivation for many years, is *Gladiolus byzantinus*. It comes from the Mediterranean, and is one of the earliest of the gladiolus to flower. In light sandy soil and full sun it is perfectly hardy, never needing to be lifted, and it also increases well. In June this has flowers of reddish-purple, and while these may lack the size and splendour of the later flowering hybrids, they bear up well without staking. The bulbous *Galtonia candicans* (see p. 120) is a good plant to succeed this.

A very beautiful close relative of the gladiolus is *Acidanthera bicolor* 'Murielae' which comes from Abyssinia. This is a bulbous plant that can be treated in the same way as the gladiolus, dried off in the winter and planted out again in April. In favourable winters we have had them spring to life again in warm well-drained places, but if the season should be a cold wet one, it makes them rather late flowering. In such positions, if planted in April, the gladiolus-

Eucomis comosa in flower by September

Eucomis comosa. Handsome leafed in late May

H. E. Bawden

Dimorphotheca ecklonis Prostrata. Snow-white, blue-violet centred flowers
from May till October

H. E. Bawden

J. R. A. Davies

Hemerocallis double variety

Schizostylis 'Mrs. Heggarty'. The valuable late-flowering pink Kaffir Lily

J. R. A. Davies

Dimorphotheca barberiae compacta. Handsome dark-centred pink daisies

Donald F. Merrett

Iris tectorum. The sun-loving roof iris of Japan

J. R. A. Davies

Thermopsis montana

Anemone tetrasepala. An unusual windflower from Kashmir

J. R. A. Davies

Lychnis dioica flore pleno. Double form of our native plant

H. E. Bawden

Oenothera glaber

like foliage appears in a few weeks. The flower stems reach 2½–3 feet, and the first blossoms usually appear in mid-August. The blooms are pure glistening white with a blackish-maroon centre, most arresting and exotic, and accompanied by a delicious scent. They have a graceful pendulous pose and make a very lovely picture with some of the highly coloured salvias; they last well into October.

A perfect little summer-flowering bulb for warm sandy soil is *Lapeyrousia cruenta*, which used to be *Anomatheca cruenta*, the latter a rather more pleasing combination of syllables. From quite a small corm, this sends up little crimson-scarlet flowers which have a darker basal blotch. The flowers are borne in mid-July upon slender 6-inch stems, and sometimes later in the summer. Lapeyrousia is often offered in the cheaper stores, and is well worth looking out for, for a dozen or so may be planted quite close together to make a bright patch.

A low-growing treasure which might well be planted near the latter is *Nierembergia repens* (syn. *N. rivularis*) which comes from Argentina but is perfectly hardy. It is a low growing carpeting plant very suitable for sunny, sandy, moist edges or pathside where it will spread rapidly. It springs to life in May with a low mat of dark green leaves. In July and almost all the summer, it sends up masses of erect, pearly-white cups as much as 2 inches across, and these are only an inch above the leaves. Running along in a mass, it is an impressive sight.

For those who like the adventure of raising plants from seed, the beautiful and unusual *Rehmannia angulata* gives reasonably quick results. It may be found in seed specialist's catalogues and is usually given as a half-hardy biennial, but in light soil and warm places may sometimes be hardy though not long lived. Belonging to the *Scrophulariaceae* family, it is very showy, sending up 2-foot stems on which are borne large, foxglove-like flowers over a long period. They are equally large, but wider at the lip than the foxglove and are coloured carmine-red. Seeds should be sown early in the year to make good sized flowering plants for the next season, but are best overwintered for the first season in frame or cold greenhouse. Incidentally it is most attractive as a pot plant for the cold greenhouse, but does not set seed under glass.

With their handsome foxglove bells, we count the penstemons among the most beautiful and colourful of the early autumn flowers. To give of their best they all need warm borders facing the sunshine. Of the hardiness of *Penstemon isophyllus* we were never certain, and have always grown it near a wall, but 1963 was a proving test, and it is still growing well. It is very lovely in the later summer months and also into October, when it is still show-ing its pendulous, salmon-red tubular flowers. Against a wall it grows up to 3 feet, yet planting space should be allowed, for at its zenith it will lean forward gracefully to display its flowers. *P. campanulatus* is also a sound perennial, a woody-stemmed little bush of 2 feet with slender, erect spikes of tapering tubular blos-soms nearly all the summer. *P. campanulatus* 'Evelyn' is a favourite with clear pink flowers, and only 12–15 inches high; both may easily be recognized by their very narrow leaves.

Yet another one is the old-timer *P. barbatus* (syn. *Chelone barbata*), up to 2½ feet; this is very distinct and handsome with airy spikes of many coral-red bugles. It is tough enough for most borders, but if the position is sunny and well drained it may well be grouped among the darker-leaved shrubs such as *Garrya elliptica* or spring-flowering shrubs which have finished bloom-ing. There are also the named hybrids, pleasing, large-leaved, shiny evergreen bushes of 2 feet, first-class, with large flowers over a long period. Two proven hardy ones are 'Garnet', deep crimson from July to October, and 'Schonholzeri' brilliant red. Any pruning or cutting out of spent growths should be left until the spring.

With these sun-lovers we include *Iris tectorum* and the Algerian *I. stylosa*. The latter, now known as *I. unguicularis*, is undoubtedly one of our most lovely winter-flowering subjects, which revels in its dry position close up to the house wall. In rich soil it is apt to make too much leaf at the expense of flowers, though once it has made a good clump and starved the position with a crowd of roots it will begin to flower more freely. Fortunately ours is in light and sandy soil, and now it is established it seems indifferent to any drought. It is a great joy to see its flowers in winter, at any time from December to April, so large and beautiful, nearly 3 inches across and almost sky blue. Though we always prefer to

see our flowers outside, there is a good excuse to enjoy them indoors at this time of year and if they are picked in bud, they soon
expand their beauty and fill the room with fragrance. Snails are
apt to find a home amidst the leaves and damage the buds, so that
it is worth while having a war upon them before flowering time.
It has always been said that *I. tectorum* grows on roofs in Japan,
but they must be of somewhat different material to ours! We much
prefer to see it at ground level where the flat outline of its exquisite flowers can be appreciated. It flowers in June and needs a
hot position and occasional division to keep it flowering freely.
After it has flowered is the best time for this, and a liberal dressing
of bonemeal helps to feed it. Foot-high stems stand well above
broad, pale green, arching leaves and the fine rich blue flowers are
white crested. These sunny situations are always in demand and
though ours is not really an iris soil, the sandy parts grow the
dwarf *pumila* irises very well. They are indispensable for their free
and early flowering and can be had in shades of yellow, gold,
white, purple and blue.

Most interesting is a bulbous iris which also does well in the
sunshine, and this is *I. bucharica* from Central Asia. It is exotic in
flower and leaf and though it belongs to the difficult Juno section
of the irises, it is a robust grower, steadily forming a compact
clump. Its time is towards the end of April when a subtle combination of soft creamy-white and yellow flowers emerge from each
of the leaf axils of its 18-inch stem; these are as many as six to
seven. This done, its hours are short, for back to rest it goes,
sometimes yielding seed from which it may readily be raised. It is
important to see that other plants do not encroach upon it when
dormant, for it still likes to sun-bathe.

The striking and unusual *Arnebia echioides* (syn. *Macrotomia
echioides*) justifies its inclusion among the special sun-lovers.
Though often occupying rock garden pockets, it is also a very
good foreground plant if it is among other choice plants that will
not rob it of its maximum sunshine, but it must be deep and well
drained soil. With these two 'ifs and buts' fulfilled, it is a sound
perennial and long-lived. First signs of life are in the spring when
a tuft of dark green leaves appear. In May and June and at other
intervals it raises foot-high stems with clusters of rich 5-petalled

yellow flowers. Each flower is marked with a black spot which gradually fades as the flowers mature. It is a Caucasian plant and rarely fails to arouse comment from discriminating visitors.

One is often lost in amazement at the indescribable beauty of flowers both large and small, and though our 'bedding out' days are long behind us, the fascination of seed raising is ever present. The climbing *Cobaea scandens* is one of the plants that we occasionally raise, a beautiful half-hardy annual that is well worth while in garden and greenhouse. Its bell-shaped flowers, getting on for Canterbury bell-size, have an impelling fascination looking down from some 7–8 feet or more, a height it will attain in a season. If seed is sown in February, plants are strong enough to plant out by late May. It can be used to grow up through any wall shrub, rose post or may serve to fill in where losses may have occurred. At the threat of winter when it would be destroyed, we often have mercy upon a plant and get one into a large pot for the greenhouse, where it will continue to bloom and will serve for the next year. Another favourite that is worth the trouble of keeping under glass is the half-hardy perennial, heliotrope, 'Cherry Pie', or *Heliotropium peruvianum* which we always like to have for its delightful scent. It never goes out before June, and its planting position is always zealously reserved—a warm corner near the house. Its quiet, pale to dark lavender flowers are reminiscent of other days, and on warm days its fragrance pervades the air around.

The tigridias also like the sunniest situations—we have rather an admiration for their gorgeous flowers which have a good range of striking colours. They are bulbous plants that should be put in in April and then lifted in the autumn and dried off like gladiolus. In our own sharply drained soil, we find they winter safely. Each sumptuous great flower is short lived, but they continue to come for many weeks.

If your garden programme does extend to trying something different now and then, and there is sunny wall space to spare, the 'Lion's-ear', *Leonotis leonurus*, is well worth trying. It is a handsome South African half-hardy perennial which parades an impressive brilliance of bright orange-scarlet in late September and into October. It is a sparkling sight, fiercely flaunting its colour with little else to compete or create a discord. On semi-shrubby stems of 2–3 feet, its flowers are carried in whorls like the phlomis to which it is closely akin. It may not flower until its second season, so that if the winter is severe it is wise to protect it with matting or bracken.

Another unusual plant is *Scilla peruviana;* its name is something of a paradox, for it does not come from Peru but from the Mediterranean and might also be found under the title of the 'Cuban lily'. It acquired its name from the fact that it was originally brought to Europe in a ship called the *Peru.* In spite of its warmer climate it is hardy and a good plant for any sunny border, and will form an interesting tuft of large fleshy, evergreen leaves. In May it sends up a large and striking umbel of hundreds of blue flowers on a foot-high stalk. It is an easy plant to grow and increases well in a fairly moist sharply drained soil and may be divided when the bulbs get too crowded.

Also with these sun-lovers there is hardly a more glorious plant to grow than the hardy nasturtium, *Tropaeolum polyphyllum.* Unfortunately of late years it has become more difficult to obtain and while it may be slow to establish in the mass, the time would come when you might curse it or bless it for its foaming beauty. Yet a tangle of its golden blossoms tumbling down a sunny bank in summer is a most wonderful sight. We have seen it used most effectively carpeting rose beds where the soil was deep and warm, the beauty of its prostrate, silvery, glaucous foliage proving a lovely foil to the roses. When received as tubers, these should be planted a good 6 inches deep, and they will pull themselves even deeper as they increase and establish. Care should be taken not to rake over the soil in the spring, for they will already be near the surface and are easily broken off.

A nasturtium which is only half-hardy is *T. tuberosum* from Peru, but it is easily managed and the tubers can be lifted in autumn and dried off in a frost-free place until planting in March. We have wintered it against a wall in mild seasons, but its large, potato-like tubers are apt to pile up too near the surface and will not stand frost. It is a climber, light and airy in growth, and does little harm scrambling up rhododendrons or other shrubs. It has glaucous-green leaves and its orange and red flowers go right on into October unless cut by frost.

The sun-loving linums are always popular for border or rock garden, but one we especially love is *Linum monogynum* from New Zealand. It is indispensable for those who like this family of quiet and graceful beauty. The blue-flowered flaxes, *L. perenne* and *L. narbonense* send up bushes of elegant wiry stems up to 2–2½ feet which are topped with salver-shaped flowers over a long season. They are plants for grouping in warm dry places for, like *L. monogynum*, they do not mind drought.

Like many New Zealand plants, *L. monogynum* has white flowers and also differs from the other linums in that its individual flowers last several days, whereas those of *L. perenne* and *L. narbonense* fall and are replenished each day. It makes an elegant little fairy bush of 9–10 inches high, many-stemmed and clothed with fresh evergreen leaves. The white salver-shaped blooms, with pointed petals, are produced in an unending succession from early June to August.

Finally among the exotics are the eucomis, a small genus of bulbous plants from South Africa. They belong to the lily family and earn their title of 'Pineapple Flowers' from the crown of leaves which grows on the top of the flower spike. As handsome foliage plants alone they are very effective, and their garden merit also is in their late flowering, their blossoms lasting as long as two months. Though only one has come our way so far, it has set us another target to obtain any that may be available. After displaying a most interesting flat rosette of 6-inch long, wavy leaves for a season or so, *Eucomis comosa* (syn. *E. punctata*) at last flowered for us in September. Its stout 2–3-foot stem bears many-flowered, creamy-white campanulate blossoms which are tinged with pink. It has been quite hardy in a warm sunny position and it is possible that others of the species may be as hardy in the south of England. They increase well and are easily raised from seed, flowering in their third or fourth year.

✳ 2 ✳
Favourite Herbaceous Perennials

Now we come to some of the perennials that we grow, including those that thrive between some of the shrubs. There is often a controversy about this, for opinions differ as to whether herbaceous perennials should be grown with shrubs. We feel that the shrubs provide a natural background to a number of plants which perhaps look out of place in the conventional border.

The shady or sun-screened side of the shrubs gives a coolness at the root and just the right setting for certain plants. The spaces and bays between the shrubs create a pseudo-woodland where they can look, and be, quite happy with the protection and dappled shade. To be seen at their best, and as plants of character, *Anemone tetrasepala*, *Diplarrhena moraea*, some of the polygonums and others, need a woodland setting. Others show up to advantage as groups to the foreground of this mixed planting. Those that like more sun are grown on the sunny side of conifers or shrubs. This interplanting gives variety in colour and shades, and a varied outline instead of monotony in the overall planting.

Since we have no time for staking and tying plants, there are few that exceed a foot or so, and these do little harm to our shrubs. Our veratrums, meconopsis and lilies are about the tallest and stand up sturdily enough in their sheltered bays among the conifers and shrubs.

Just as roses, lavenders, delphiniums and many other plants have earned themselves a place in most gardens, so the phloxes deserve their niche for their long season of bloom and their fragrance. Unfortunately, they do not like our acid soil overmuch, but their valuable time of blossoming, from mid-June, earns them space for a few named varieties here and there. There is no doubt that they need plenty of moisture and feeding. Our modest successes are in a border which does not receive the fullest sun. They are wonderful plants when seen at their best and may be chosen at any nursery or horticultural show.

The phlox that has gained a certain place in garden design and as a spectacular contrast plant is the variety 'Norah Leigh'. The effect of its variegation of green and pale yellow stands out prominently from a distance, and it is outstanding in contrast to dark foliage or violet-purple flowers such as the spikes of *Salvia nemerosa* 'Superba' (syn. *S. virgata* 'Nemorosa'). Its flowers are purple, but of little consequence in relation to its foliage effect.

One of our favourites of the species is *P. maculata* from North America. Unlike the border phlox, the flowers are in long pyramidal clusters and consequently very showy, especially in a group. The fragrant blossoms are a rich mauve-pink, long lasting, and are borne in late June. It is long-lived and indestructible, slowly spreading into a thick clump. While not suffering from the drawbacks of the border phlox, it responds to generous treatment and a fairly moist position. There is a white form of it which is also most desirable and proves to be an equally good doer in moist soil.

Generally, *Anemone narcissiflora* is regarded as 'among the alpines', for it graces the high alpine meadows of a number of countries, but with us it is a good-tempered perennial in any well-drained place. It lives among our dwarf shrubs and it seems to appreciate the coolness at the root, for it sends up 18-inch stems peeping over the top with an array of lovely apple-blossom-like flowers in May. That it stands up and looks after itself, also having its own 'home-made' colony from seed, makes it a good garden plant that might well be seen more in gardens. If seed be needed for sowing, it must be watched carefully, for it may be taken green and when it comes away easily.

Another anemone that can be on the selected list for the busy gardener who requires carefree and interesting plants that do not need staking, is *A. tetrasepala*. This comes from Kashmir and is a reliable free flowering perennial, non-invasive, and demanding very little in the way of cultivation. Very large, dark green leaves characterize it as a handsome plant, and these begin to unfold in late spring; then from the axils of the leaves the flowering stems rise to almost 2 feet. Though individually not very large, the flowers are very numerous, and it presents an elegant cluster of pure white flowers with the undersides of the petals shaded pink. In mid-May, against the dark green leaves they are very effective and last for many weeks before they begin their function of setting seed. The shadier side of the border should be chosen, but if it is possible, moist soil at the woodland or streamside is the perfect setting for its character. Seed germinates well and plants will often start to bloom in their second year.

For moist places in sunshine, one of the hardiest of the verbenas, *V. corymbosa*, always gives pleasure because of the flower likeness to the bedding heliotrope, and also because of its similar fragrance. Forming a compact mat of dark evergreen leaves, it sends up erect 18-inch stems on which its terminal heads of pale lavender flowers are carried from mid-July until late autumn. These stems are very wiry and need no looking after, and in other ways it cares for itself by rooting and seeding mildly; it can be rampageous when well suited.

The perennial lobelias, too, are moisture lovers, and here we grow *Lobelia syphilitica*, which is erect and up to 2–2½ feet, a late flowerer which fends for itself and needs no stakes. Though not often seen, it has been in cultivation for a long time and though for some it might lack the glowing high coloured effect of *L. cardinalis*, it scores in being quite hardy, long-lived and standing quite a lot of neglect. Its rosette of dark evergreen leaves can be easily pulled to pieces in spring or early autumn and the divisions set to best effect in sizeable groups. It flowers for many weeks from mid-summer onwards, giving subdued light blues, lavender, purple and pink and even a white form, all of which will furnish self-sown seedlings.

At last the day lilies (*Hemerocallis*) with their lily-like flowers, are getting more recognition as good garden plants for the beauty of flowers and foliage. This is greatly due to an immense improvement in the colour range, length of flowering time and to the increase in demand for labour saving plants. With many shades of yellow, rich orange, mahogany-reds, salmon-pinks, creamy-pinks and many variations, there is an array of named cultivars in catalogues which should satisfy all tastes. Though liking moisture and responding accordingly with lush foliage and longer flowering stems, they are most accommodating plants, doing well in any ordinary soil in sun or part shade. Together with the hostas, they are one of our allies in our fight against sorrel, which is one of our worst enemies.

In spite of investing in some of the newer hemerocallis, we still find place for *H. fulva* which has been cultivated since 1576. Its graceful, fresh green foliage is always welcome so early in the year when little else is astir. It is in June that its great 4-inch wide, orange-red flowers, upturned for inspection on sturdy 3–4-foot stems are seen at their best. Its double form, *H. fulva* 'Kwanso' *flore pleno* is unusual, handsome and vigorous with very large flowers of orange-buff; neither of these need any support.

There are other species, too, which have their charm, *H. nana* is among these, no less indestructible and one of the earliest to bloom. Less lush, more grassy in foliage, but with fairly large yellow flowers on 18–24-inch stems, it takes a place near the front of shrubs. Beginning to flower by early May, it continues till the end of June. *H. thunbergii*, another small compact species also flowering about mid-May, has trumpet flowers of apricot-yellow on 2–2½-foot stems.

Also taking its place among the shrub bays is *Diplarrhena moraea*, a fascinating Tasmanian which we usually refer to as the 'Giraffe Plant'. Its glistening, marble-white 3-petalled flowers, beautifully marked with gold and mauve, are held stiffly on 2-foot stems. With two of the three petals uppermost, rather like giraffe's ears, it seems even more fascinating peering into the fading light of the evening, as though intrigued with its adopted country. These beautiful, orchid-like flowers are put forth in a continuous succession from June into August, never marred by wind or rain. We have grown this for many years and found it absolutely hardy, well deserving of its title, the 'Poor Man's Orchid'. With stiff evergreen foliage, not unlike the Gladwyn iris, it is attractive in the winter time. It has done exceptionally well in our peaty soil and succeeds best in reasonably moist soil or with slight shade, steadily increasing its clump year by year. The dwarf alpine form,

D. moraea 'Alpina', is most desirable for the rock garden, and forms a close grassy tuft with white flowers on 4–5-inch stems.

As well as for the border, some of the campanulas, too, are useful for grouping among the shrubs. Two of our own native plants, the enduring *Campanula trachelium* and *C. latifolia* 'Macrantha' being worthy of such places, as well as in the wild garden. In a world of newer plants, the latter, our own noble bell-flower of northern woodlands, has much to recommend it. It stands up sturdily to 3–4 feet, scorning pea sticks and stakes, and then from mid-June to early July bears huge drooping bells of violet-purple, almost as large as Canterbury bells. In case violet-purple should offend, its white form is supreme and may be seen in stately, magnificent clumps in the wood at the Royal Horticultural Society's Garden at Wisley. We always have this admiration for our own natives, and the 2-foot *C. trachelium* of Sussex and Surrey waysides, though not in the top rank, plays its part in odd corners, giving large bells of deep purple to whites, with all shades of purple in between.

The handsome-leaved *C. alliariifolia* from the Caucasus is hearty enough to fend for itself, and produces 2-inch long, creamy-white bells in June to July. It naturally flops forward and can be used somewhere near the front of the border or as ground-cover, using a number of plants round about shrubs. Undoubtedly one of the finest of the tall bellflowers is *C. lactiflora*, another Caucasian. In our days of perennial borders in the old cottage garden it fitted in well with the back-benchers, but though fairly rigid, it usually had to be supported.

Baptisia australis came along with a host of other removals, old favourites, plants that had associations, gifts from gardeners past and present, and ones that had been cosseted to life from the merest sprig and to be looked forward to at a future date. It is unusual, as from its lupin-like appearance, one might hazard that it would have yellow or pink flowers, but they turn out to be that rare colour in the garden, having rich blue, pea flowers on long spikes. It is a member of a small genus from the United States and makes a graceful light foliaged plant for a sunny mixed border. It grows up to 3 feet, and being rather leafy, it seems to catch the wind and generally needs staking.

Yet another uncommon lupin-like perennial for the sunny border is *Thermopsis montana* from the United States, likewise of the *Leguminosae* family. It gives a very cheerful note to the May–June border, sending up 18–24-inch spikes of yellow pea flowers. When established it spreads rather rapidly, but has the merit of holding itself erect.

The trusty *Coreopsis verticillata* has always found a place in our borders and now fills in odd corners as ground-cover and a weed smotherer. Few weeds ever penetrate its massed roots and thickets of stems, and it is one of the jolliest of medium height flowering plants. These perennials that crop up year after year, giving so much without needing any care, give us time for the extra that others need. *C. verticillata* produces its golden-yellow, starry flowers in a mass from June till the end of August.

There is a fair selection of these trouble-free, upstanding plants, *Liatris spicata* falling into this category. It is a very worth-while plant that is easily obtained as dry tubers in the spring from garden departments of numerous stores. They may look rather shrivelled clumps but soon establish, though care must be taken to plant them the right way up. Liatris carries on from year to year, sending up a fluffy, feathery, rosy-purple spike of bloom some 2½ feet high. It is rather an odd child of the *Compositae* family, but is striking in effect, with its flowers packed closely on the spike, flowering from the top downwards, lasting for many weeks of July. To avoid any colour clash this grows alongside *Thermopsis montana*, with the autumn-flowering sedums quite near to follow on.

How these autumn-flowering sedums have been improved, indeed our old friend the pink-headed *Sedum spectabile* so loved by the hovering butterflies is one of the joys of the autumn, together with its named rosy-pink cultivars 'Carmen' and 'Brilliant', and the almost red 'Meteor'. These are all no-trouble plants, being content in practically any soil in full sun. From late spring onwards their large fleshy, glaucous leaves are decorative, and at 12–15 inches in height, their great flat heads of bloom, composed of myriads of small flowers, are ideal for foreground planting. In places where the soil is more retentive, the incredible blue of *Gentiana sino-ornata* alongside is a perfect colour combination. *S.*

telephium, a native plant, and one that we were thrilled to find already growing here in sandy places, also takes its place between plants. We have our soft spot for most natives, and though it may not catch everybody's eye, it is nevertheless worthy of the small space it occupies. At first rising it shows fleshy, glaucous-green leaves, but these change to a purplish tinge as the foot-long stems bear their dull red heads of flowers. The form *S. telephium* 'Roseum Variegatum' we value even more, partly for its new growth of pink, and pink heads of flowers but also the fact that it was given to us by that notable alpine gardener, the late Mr Walter Ingwersen.

For those who want something more flamboyant, the newer hybrid, *S. telephium* 'Autumn Joy' is a grand plant and so well named, besides having a decorative value for a very long period when it has finished flowering. This is a fine strong grower with flat heads of rose-salmon on 2-foot stems; there is also *S. telephium* 'Munstead Red', a dark red. *S. maximum* 'Atropurpureum' is of course one of the flower arranger's dreams, with leaves and stems of a rich mahogany-red. It is a handsome plant, bearing loose heads of pale pink flowers earlier in July; its only fault is that heavy rain or hail can spot the leaves and marr them. *S. maximum* 'Versicolor' is brilliant yellow, edged green, with stems very slightly pink and is a good plant to contrast with the latter or any dark leaved mat-forming subject.

The anaphalis are also for sunshine and dry places, and their silvery-grey foliage is very precious for showing up other plants. Though of the daisy family, the flowers are by no means typical, and might be mistaken for those of many of the helichrysums. Their flower composition is in branching heads of fluffy, white everlasting flowers, which last a long time when cut for decoration. *Anaphalis margaritacea* and *A. yedoensis* are erect growing, up to 18–20 inches, and stand up well, the latter especially so. *A. triplinervis* is the star turn, a stay-at-home plant, compact and ideal for the border edge. With a silvery-whiteness about its broad foliage, this forms a flat rosette upon the ground, and besides being so ornamental, is one of the best of low ground-covering perennials. July and into the late autumn is its flowering time, when its white flowers are held on branching heads 10–12 inches above the foliage. It differs from the others in preferring a moister soil and is accommodating in being quite happy with a modicum of shade.

Monarda didyma, with the lovely name of bergamot, gives the splendid colour that is always associated with border pictures. It is an old-time plant and has always been a must with us, and causes perhaps the few occasions when we envy those with rich moist soils where it is always seen to perfection. After losses in our lighter soil, partial shade from trees has been the answer to holding a little moisture for it. With a carpet of primulas and a backing of the *sibirica* irises, we can now regard it with some satisfaction and without reproach. Being only a surface rooter, it benefits by occasional division and replanting in spring. A year may often be gained by topdressing with good soil, either is an easy and pleasant task, for its leaves are strongly aromatic. Flowering from June onwards, its close heads of rich, vivid scarlet are most effective. Note should be made of others such as 'Croftway Pink' rose-pink, 'Burgundy' dark purple, and a variety of other shades, which, with *M. didyma* itself, all reach some 2½–3 feet.

A plant that associates well with the bergamot is the 'Whorl Flower', *Morina longifolia*. Although introduced from the Himalayas more than a hundred years ago, it is only in recent years that it has become better known. In spite of its origin it has proved a good perennial and, being evergreen, it should be grown for its ornamental thistle-like foliage, as well as for its bold and striking appearance when in flower. Arising from the tuft of long spiny leaves, the 3-foot stems carry whorls of tubular flowers in the late summer. The elongated blossoms, which are wider at the mouth, open a pale pink and fade to white, and are borne round the stems in a long succession from June to July. It looks in keeping standing up at the margins of pool or stream, as long as it is in sunshine. It is easily raised from seed and plants may be put out while quite young, and will often bloom in their third year.

Other perennials of the moist border, but whose rightful and natural place is by the waterside, are the lythrums, those improved forms of *Lythrum salicaria*, the purple loosestrife which so enrich and colour our streamsides and ditches with their haze of purple in July and August. They grow freely enough in any good garden soil, making splendid, non-staking, gay, carefree plants varying from 3-4 feet in height, and are always worth planting in a group. One of the older cultivars, 'Rose Queen', can still hold its own among the best. 'Lady Sackville', 'Brightness' and the 'Beacon' are tall growing, and 'Robert' is a very good medium grower.

For sunny places the asphodels, known as the 'King's Spear', are perhaps the least cultivated of the lily family, and though *Asphodeline lutea* (syn. *Asphodelus luteus*) was first introduced some 300-400 years ago, it is very rarely seen in gardens. It is not by reason of any difficulty in cultivation, for it is by no means particular as to soil and it forms quite lusty clumps in time. It is admirable at all seasons, in winter especially, and its attractive basal cluster of thin grey-green, grassy leaves provide a good contrast to other plants in the border. At mid-border, but not lost among taller plants, its unbranched spike of 3 feet is ornamentally distinct, with a pleasing inflorescence of bright yellow. The flowers are in a long 18-inch raceme, opening from the top downwards, and are noticeably fragrant. It has thong-like roots which may easily be divided in the spring or early autumn if the clump becomes overcrowded. Though succeeding in dryish sunny places, it responds to generous treatment and plenty of moisture.

The rudbeckias do well in almost any soil, but preferably on the moist side. While the tall ones such as *Rudbeckia purpurea* (now more correctly, *Echinacea purpurea*) and its named cultivars have a great appeal, for trouble-free gardening we have always grown R. *speciosa* which maintains its 2 feet without any help from us. The large golden-rayed daisies of this plant, with their closely packed central disk of black, which earns it the title of 'Black-eyed Susan', make it one of the most handsome of the near-the-front July to August performers. The last named is always an effective plant, but the newer R. 'Goldsturm' is a great improvement in size of bloom and quality. Years ago an old gardener gave us sound advice when he remarked that it was always best to get a named variety of any plant. In a few years there may be many more exceptionally fine and large flowered cultivars of these rudbeckias.

The tradescantias go well alongside the latter, for they also have a general height of 2 feet and their foliage is interesting, rush-like and arching and breaks the ground quite early in the season, some of it with a pinky tinge which turns green as the plants develop. Had we room for more borders we would grow a few more, for their value lies in permanence, and the minimum of cultural attention. Though theirs is a quiet beauty, the tradescantias bloom from June to September. The white flowered 'Osprey' and deep blue 'Kreisler' are all we grow, but with the old-time ones so much improved there are many to choose from.

As much as some plants love our acid peaty soil, we have to face the fact that the exotic peonies are not, so far, one of our successes; years more of cultivation may gradually neutralize it for plants like these. We know a little lime would help, but in such a mixed planting we dare not do so. It is true that the majority we moved in big clumps, whereas young divisions have done better. For instance *Paeonia veitchii woodwardii* were young plants which now occupy spaces between shrubs and are happy enough. We have a special regard for this species for it is distinguished by its low clump of finely cut fern-like foliage and its dwarf habit which makes it very suitable to grow near the border edge. It is easy-going and a generous flowerer, bearing several flowers to a stem. These are lovely single blossoms of soft rose-pink in early June Another dwarf, and an aristocrat of these wild peonies is *cambessedesii* from the Balearic Islands. One of the earliest to flower, sometimes before the end of April, its 3-inch wide, cup-shaped flowers are a lovely shade of pink, variable to deep pink in some. In foliage alone it holds a place, with specially colourful leaves, glossy silvery-green with mahogany undersides. So choice is this, that the rock garden is one of the best havens, or between some choice dwarf shrubs, and then it should be well caressed by the sun.

So beautiful is *P. obovata* 'Alba' that few could resist the charm of its great pure white goblets, or rest until they have obtained a plant! Further enhanced with golden stamens and a crimson centre, its beauty is quite heavenly. Though it only bears one blossom to each 2–2½-foot stem, it has ample lobed foliage of soft bronze-green in perfect harmony to add to its merit. If the blossoms have any fault, it is that they are fleeting and their 'precious hours' must not be missed.

Another must for those who plant peonies is the rare *P.*

mlokosewitschii, a superb tempter for the exchequer! It is a marvellous Caucasian species with great single, pure yellow blossoms on 2-foot stems, and as with almost all of them, splendid foliage. We are assured that this is an easy and contented plant, but so far it has not bloomed. Another to turn one's head is *P. emodii*, ravishing, with immense glistening white flowers standing well above the leaves. It is also rare, but was seed-raised and flowered in its fifth year, several flowers on 2½-foot stems.

Our tale of these is all too short, but if they are by no means cheap to buy, at least they are most rewarding in their quality and give nothing short of one's lifetime in pleasure and grandeur. Strange to say, our tree peonies described in our book of shrubs, do much better than the herbaceous ones, but we are ever optimistic and look for better things to come. Besides the species, there are the old cottage garden peonies, the cultivars of *P. officinalis*, mostly double flowers of great substance which may be seen in flower in their great variety at any nursery which specializes in them. One such which we fell for was *P. officinalis* 'Anemonaeflora Rosea', a charmer of a foot in height in rosy-pink with laciniated petals. Though one can be tempted by many, some of the older cultivars are still first-class; among so many, such names as 'Festiva Maxima', 'Karl Rosenfeld', 'Lady Alexandra Duff', 'Marie Crousse' and 'Sarah Bernhardt' can always be recommended.

Two unusual and easily grown clematis which are not climbers and may be used in the border are *Clematis recta* and *C. heracleifolia* 'Davidiana'. *C. recta* is quite an old garden plant, but not often seen. It is a splendid mid to back border plant which forms an erect bushy mass of 3 feet, upon which are a foam of long-lasting white flowers during June and July. A large plant is conspicuous and a good foil to other colours in the border. It stands up fairly well but is worth supporting with pea sticks. *C. heracleifolia* 'Davidiana' is a visitor's 'guess plant', the answer often accepted with some disbelief, for its flowers are more penstemon-like or hyacinth-like in shape. Its chief merit is a late July to September flowering period, when it produces a succession of inch-long dark blue fragrant flowers, also at just over 2 feet it does not require staking.

Another late flowerer that can be recommended is *Physostegia* 'Vivid', the Obedient Plant. Placed fairly near the front of the border, its curious obedient habit can be demonstrated to interested visitors, for when the flowers are moved they will stay in any position. At 2–2½ feet, its erect spikes require no staking and are well set with sprays of attractive rose-carmine, tubular flowers. It can be a bit of a wanderer, and when too obstreperous can be lifted in spring and its thongy roots pushed together to make a more compact plant.

Another wanderer is *Saponaria officinalis* 'Flore Pleno' (more correctly *S. o.* 'Rosea-plena') with the epithet of 'Bouncing Bet', which well describes its hearty habits when pleased with its diet. But its other title of 'Goodbye to Summer', gives the clue to the months of August and September when its soft pink flowers send out the most delicious of scents. It is an old-world garden favourite that grows wild in Sussex waysides and maybe other places. For all its untidy manner of growth, 18 inches to 2 feet of flopping stems, we love it and have always had it in some odd sunny or semi-shady position. At times you may have to declare war upon it to give others the pleasure of some pieces, but it is unlikely that you will win the battle if it is really well established —it will be better to lose!

One plant which we never seem to lose is *Lychnis coronaria*, the rose campion, *Agrostemma coronaria* being its old name. Though individual plants do not live long, even if we have not deliberately moved it with us, its seeds are usually carried with some other plant. One associates its rosette of silvery, woolly leaves with old gardens, so long has it been in cultivation, and though its flowers may be accused of being magenta, its performance is brilliant. There are also forms such as *L. coronaria* 'Atrosanguinea' with dark crimson flowers. It grows up to 2–2½ feet and flowers between July and August.

Gaura lindheimeri is one of those plants which is graceful and elegant of habit. As its flights of flowers are never too many at once, it helps to relieve any heavier planting, or mass of flowers. It is slender in build, with light branching stems which bear racemes of pink buds opening to white. They open a few at a time, but carry on from July to August; it grows up to 3–4 feet.

It is surprising how many of the South African plants are hardy in this country, a notable and well tried one being *Phygelius capensis*, the Cape figwort, which has been grown in Britain for well over a hundred years. It comes under the heading of useful late flowerers, beginning in early August and going on into the late autumn. It has penstemon-like flowers which stand up well above the foliage, handsome, almost exotic, and in colourful panicles of tubular, 2-inch long flowers of coral-red. While this is also quite a good wall shrub, where it may grow up to 5–6 feet, it always seems to be happier in a moist sunny border where it will make a bushy 3-foot mound. Whereas most gardeners know the former, *P. aequalis* is less common, yet well worth obtaining, for there is a warmth in its beautiful colouring. It is also more effective, as the drooping flowers are held more closely to the spike, there are many more of them, and they are larger. The soft salmon-rose, yellowish within the flower, is a subtle combination of colours. It is also quite hardy and grows up to 2½–3 feet.

Though *Geranium anemonifolium* may not have a good reputation for being hardy or long-lived in some soils, it is undoubtedly unique in many ways. Its glossy evergreen leaves alone are an asset, like some giant herb robert, but it is so refined and glorious in flower that losses are always worth replacing. So easily raised from seed, it makes strong flowering plants very quickly, also sowing itself. From June onwards the flowers are borne in great abundance on stems which rise up well over the leaves to a height of 2–2½ feet. The flowers are fully open, a soft, satiny rose deepening to a darker coloured eye, the flower stems being tinted with purplish hairs. It is not a plant for a cold wet soil but for warm favourable parts, then individual plants will last some years, by which time they will have sown themselves. Though it can be effective in a border, it is best for the wild part of the garden, and it will prosper in sun or shade. Some of the best we have seen have prospered for years at the foot of a hedge, evidently sheltered and kept dry in the winter.

Geranium lowei is another distinct species comparable with the foregoing. It has great big evergreen, shiny leaves, a heartening sight in winter, and then in the summer, many branching stems carry the rosy-purple blossoms. For a really glorious patch of

colour, *G. psilostemon*, often known as *G. armenum*, can be a real
eye-opener when it is in full flower in June. It rarely grows much
over 2½ feet and forms a dome of broad, deeply lobed leaves which
colour well in the autumn. Above this handsome foliage, the
bowl-shaped flowers are borne in great profusion. The blossoms
are an inch across, an intense magenta-crimson, accentuated by a
black centre and black veining of the petals. It is perfectly hardy
and robust in any sunny well-drained soil.

Most of us keep our old-timers, and with us it has always been
a leaning towards plants with penstemon-like flowers. Such is
Penstemon barbatus, at one time known as *Chelone barbata*, and having spikes of narrow scarlet tubes in June. Unless carefully placed
in a border its colour can be difficult to tone in, but it is often
more effective grouped in a sunny position between shrubs where
its tapering, yard-high stems look very graceful; it is a sound
perennial. *Chelone obliqua* is quite different and deserving more
recognition for the unusual charm of blossom in its soft rose. It is
sturdier than *Penstemon barbatus*, with stiff, erect stems of almost
3 feet, and the flowers are very large, plump and antirrhinum-like,
flowering from July to August.

Also erect growing and one of the tallest of the family is the
uncommon *Linaria dalmatica*, an attractive toadflax with glaucous-
blue foliage. Raising slender 3–3½-foot stems, this is a good fill-in
for the sunny border and easily placed by reason of its light and
airy form, and its long racemes of clear yellow flowers which tone
with almost anything. It flowers continuously from May till
September and, conveniently, sows itself.

Many of the polygonums are coarse and invasive, but two that
we always find room for are *Polygonum bistorta* 'Superbum' and *P.
amplexicaule* 'Speciosum'. Both are easily grown and need plenty
of room in the moist parts of the border or semi-wild garden.
P. bistorta 'Superbum' we presume to be a superior form of our
own charming native plant which peeps up pretty pink spikes by
moist roadsides. It is a very fine form for the garden, sending up a
clump of large dock-like leaves in late spring and is in flower by
the end of May, with handsome bottle-brush heads of soft pink
on 18-inch stems. *P. amplexicaule* 'Speciosum' forms a leafy clump,
but needs room as the slender flowering stems develop and spray

around. From the end of June right into the autumn, it sends out masses of wiry stems which bear poker-heads of deep rosy-crimson, very useful for cutting and adding to posies of flowers.

Those who like the Jerusalem sage (*Phlomis fruticosa*), will also appreciate the form of the herbaceous *P. viscosa*, which is so valuable for its large wrinkled leaves. It is one of those medium height border plants that makes a bold foreground plant as a foil to small plants and helps to relieve too regular a formation of planting in the front row. It forms a neat, flat rosette with its big rough leaves, and sends up stout 3-foot flower stems which bear whorls of soft yellow flowers at intervals up the stem from June to July.

One more plant which qualifies to go with these favourite perennials is *Lychnis dioica flore pleno*, another old-timer, the double form of a native plant, sometimes included in the genus *Melandrium*. This is a useful mid-border one, standing up nice and erect at 2 feet with showy and sizeable rosy-cerise flowers in June. It makes a good leafy clump which is easily divided if it should become less free flowering.

✳ 3 ✳

A Few Front-Line Perennials

WHAT WE CALL our front-row border plants are a miscellaneous collection of herbaceous perennials and rock plants, the latter being kinds which will stand the rough and tumble of an ordinary well-drained border. These foreground plants are mostly selected favourites of a few inches to a foot or so in height, ones that might well be used in any midget border. They are chosen because they do not need staking and most of them ask little or no attention in the way of periodical division. We find it important to have a certain number of these low growers to the fore of any border in the front of shrubs, partly as ground-cover and also to facilitate stepping over to attend to any taller ones. Clumps of plants with evergreen or striking foliage enhance the taller growers. Compactness of form here and there is as important as plants with grassy and spiky leaves, and the blending of others with different types of foliage.

Even winter has its compensations, the outlook is so different, and the picture is more fully unfolded with many plants gone to rest, so that the evergreen perennials stand out more intimately, and we see room for improvements. Bereft of leaves, the shrubs stand out more prominently—should we prune out exuberant growths that threaten some treasures, or should we move them forward to safety? These and many others are the pleasures and tasks that winter reveals.

As one of the evergreens, a Japanese treasure of the lily family, *Liriope graminifolia* (*Ophiopogon spicatus*) is a favourite, and effective in taking away that dead and sere look of the remainder of those at rest. While these sleep, liriope displays life with long dark, gracefully curving clusters of leaves, shining through any of winter's onslaughts. As a foliage plant alone it earns its place, but its 12-inch spikes of lavender-blue, closely packed, bead-like flowers are most welcome in late August, and these keep peeping up through the grassy clump right into October. Though flowering all the more freely in full sun, it will succeed in part shade. Its leafy shape lends itself to being used for paving or rock garden, spring division is the best time and way for increasing it. Another member of this interesting group is *Ophiopogon japonicus*, also from Japan and China. It is a much smaller plant, evergreen and very hardy, and has short narrow, dark green leaves which are prostrate to the ground. It spreads by creeping rhizomes, making an excellent carpeting plant for half-shady places among dwarf shrubs, or more for intimate corners and bays where smaller treasures are congregated. In June it has quaint, nodding white bells on 4-inch racemes which are followed by little black fruits in the autumn.

As the flowers of *Liriope graminifolia* are late, an earlier performer is placed nearby—this is *Oenothera glaber*, whose green rosettes in winter-time turn to an attractive red-purple in the spring. It flowers in June, giving an arresting display of very luminous, brilliant yellow cups on stiff 15–18-inch stems. One more with this arresting change of colour to its leafy rosettes in the spring is *O. cinaeus* which turns a brilliant scarlet for a few weeks. Its red buds open to golden-yellow cups. There is always something thrilling about all these evening primroses, the freedom of their flowers which glow so full of life. However, *O. glaber*, unlike quite a few, opens its flowers in the daytime, as does *O. fruticosa* 'Youngii'. The latter is yet another of 18 inches, which parades its shiny yellow cups in June. *O. fruticosa* 'Yellow River', and other named forms only differ in their shades of yellow. These make clumps of glossy-leaved rosettes of evergreen and may be planted fairly close together. All may be divided in early autumn or spring.

While the foregoing do better where it is not too dry, *O. tetragona* 'Riparia' will often thrive in drier places, more generally found in the rock garden, and it can be a useful variety for some positions in paving. Wherever it may be it puts forth tumbling masses of drooping branches which carry a glorious and long succession of clear golden blooms throughout the summer. *O. missourensis* (syn. *O. macrocarpa*) is likewise a dual purpose plant, first-class and very long lived. Being a tap-rooting plant, it likes the soil well drained, and once established it sends out many trailing shoots which loll upon the ground and send up enormous, pale yellow, upturned goblets. Starting in July, about the same time as the astonishing *O. acaulis* it flowers unceasingly till autumn. Dying down in late autumn, it does not come to life again until May. Occasionally seed is set, but it is mostly increased by summer cuttings.

The euphorbias are a vast race of plants, some weedy, others handsome, quite a few of architectural value, and many evergreen; altogether it is a fascinating genus which grows on one. A few are for the border edges, among them *Euphorbia myrsinites* which is first-class and well deserving of its Award of Merit. It bears the bluest of glaucous foliage on foot-long growths which trail and lie upon the ground, succulent and cactus-like, unhardy looking, but remaining evergreen and unperturbed by winter. In the spring these growths terminate in heads of yellow flowers which last for many weeks. It is a plant of real character and, with its tumbling irregular growths, imparts an air of informality to its allotted space. It is equally a distinctive plant for a large rock garden or rock border and is easily raised from seed.

For its masses of bright yellow, *E. epithymoides* (syn. *E. polychroma*) is an indispensable plant for the spring border. It is more formal, a tidy compact plant of 6–8 inches, flowering for many weeks before the blooms fade to green, the whole plant remaining green until it dies away in late autumn. Another dwarf plant which we used to have in the border is *E. segetalis* (syn. *E. portlandica*), a rare native perennial of a few inches, and one which is worth seeking. Its greenish flowers come in June, and it is known as the Portland spurge. The Cypress spurge, *E. cyparissias* qualifies with its dwarf habit, but can be rather invasive and is safer and quite happy in those difficult places under and around trees. In the autumn it goes a wonderful yellow shade.

Also with succulent glaucous foliage, and not unlike the euphorbias, is *Sedum roseum* (syn. *S. rhodiola*), a native of the mountains of the north of England and Scotland. It is also known as rose root, owing to its woody root having the perfume of roses. With a curious appeal, perhaps as a collector's plant and for those who love our native flora, it may not be the plant for those who are looking for a brilliant floral display. Perhaps if it were rampageous and took our time to curb it, we might not give it room, but it occupies little space and needs no care. From its thick woody rootstock it sends up erect 10–12-inch leafy stems in spring, which terminate in compact cymes of greenish-yellow flowers. As it is so easily placed, it fills in odd corners and suitable places where the merest inch or so of soil needs planting. As a friend once remarked after a contemplative glance around the garden, 'My word, you do not waste much space,' but it is all these oddments that help to make a garden interesting at all times.

Among the veronicas there is a whole host of mat-forming and useful front-row plants, in fact if there were room, one could have a whole bed devoted to them and have colour and foliage effect for a very long period, especially if some of the shrubby ones were included as well. Most outstanding for winter effect is *V. sumilensis* which makes a hearty patch of green. To the interested plantsman this is the most unusual and arouses curiosity with its tufts of stiff dark leaves which lie upon the ground like some species of baby yucca. While this is almost satisfying enough, it also sends up 6–8-inch spikes of soft blue flowers early in May, and on and off throughout the season. *V. spicata* is a native plant and its slender, bright blue 12–18-inch spires of bloom are most welcome in July and August, together with its white form. Both are small, neat foliaged, non-invasive plants which die back in winter time. It is a variable plant but has been much improved with colour forms of rose-pink in 'Barcarolle', 'Blue Peter', deep blue, 'Pavane', deep rose, and others all of a foot or more, looking very charming in a group.

Another of this clan is *V. crassifolia*, with a winter rosette of broad dark leaves, and late summer spikes of thinly tapering dark blue flowers, this is 18 inches high. The resting tufts of the broad, glossy-leaved *V. gentianoides* indeed suggest some exciting gentian, but it proves to be one of the earliest of the veronicas to flower. It sends up elegant spires of 18 inches which are set with the palest china-blue flowers. The graceful structure of its spikes provides the basic material for the effective grouping of plants for the smallest of gardens. Its variegated form, streaked with silver, is also pretty among any array of darker leaved plants.

Contrast plants are always at a premium, especially low growing ones, and *V. teucrium* 'Trehane' is quite prostrate in its habit, useful for the border of rock garden. Growing almost anywhere, in spring it is brilliantly golden-yellow, later topped by short spikes of sapphire-blue. Keeping its yellow foliage well into the summer, it is an admirable foil for almost any of the small border plants. To add to this brief selection of speedwells, the mat forming, small dark-leaved *V. prostrata* (syn. *V. rupestris*), is one of the most valuable and free growing. Its blaze of rich sapphire-blue, mere inches off the ground, almost rivals the blue of the gentians. In raised beds where the drainage may be especially good, *V. incana* is pleasant to look at all the year, well dressed with handsome leaves of silver-white. Close-set 12-inch spikes of purple contrast exceptionally well with its foliage.

In spite of so many new plants, sometimes in an almost confusing throng, some of the old ones never lose their place. One is *Stachys lanata*, the woolly-leaved lamb's ears, which grows well almost anywhere except in our peaty soil. It is most important for its big clumps of large, silvery, downy foliage which forms a striking low foundation at the border edge and helps to accentuate more colourful flowers. Even more silvery and silky is *S. lanata* 'Olympica', though the flowers are insignificant, both of these are evergreen and perfect ground-cover in front of roses.

Stachys macrantha (syn. *Betonica grandiflora*) may also be used with the roses, and is a much more showy plant as regards its flowers. It forms solid clumps of dark hairy leaves, and sends up numerous stiff spikes of 12-18 inches, on which are whorls of tubular flowers of rosy-purple to reddish-purple in May.

For contrast alongside the latter one can grow the dwarf *Doronicum cordatum* which comes from the Alps. Though more of a rock garden plant, it does well enough in an ordinary sunny border, provided it is fairly sharply drained and reasonably moist. With 2-inch wide golden daisies on 6-inch stems, which lengthen considerably as the flowers come out, it lasts for several weeks, often blooming later in the season as well. Flowering at the beginning of May, it is certainly one of the aristocrats of the family. Its leafy clump goes to rest in winter time, and benefits from an occasional replant in fresh soil. It may leave a summer gap, but there are plenty of small plants which fill in to make this less noticeable. Such late flowerers as *Amsonia salicifolia* or the dwarf polygonums would be fitting, or *Borago laxiflora* may be planted close to flop its harmless flowering stems where it may. The latter plant a Corsican, with the daintiest of azure bells, it is a borage which happens to fit in almost anywhere. While its interesting flat rosette of rough leaves takes up so little room, the thin trailing stems flop around or rise up into other small plants or shrubs and produce an endless picture of starry blue flowers from June onwards. Free with self-sown seedlings, quite one of its best and admired efforts was at the foot of the shrubby *Potentilla forrestii* and the dwarf rose 'Little White Pet', on to which the slender flower stems clung and did their charming piece.

The graceful *Amsonia salicifolia* which we had always grown so well, has not yet given of its best, and we shall probably have to re-start with a new young plant. It is a charming North American which flowers at the end of the summer, giving pale blue, periwinkle-like flowers on willowy 18-inch wands. This and *A. tabernaemontana*, which differs very little, and of which *salicifolia* may in fact be a variety, have their quiet appeal for those who like something out of the ordinary.

The polygonums take their place among the carpeters and ground coverers, where their robust clumps can be put to special purpose and restrained as necessary. However, the newer *Polygonum affine* 'Donald Lowndes' seems perfect for the front of the border, being slow growing, compact and with close spreading mats of short 4-6-inch spikes of clear pink flowers from August onwards, which all make it a very good plant to go with the autumn gentians.

The spring flowering *Gentiana acaulis* (more correctly now *G. excisa*) is another good small plant which can be used as a change and as an evergreen fill-up, for it is worth trying in any places that might bring forth its wonderful blue trumpets. Nothing is more satisfactory than to get even a few of its dazzling blue flowers. Though our autumn gentians give us a sea of blue, we cannot yet claim this for *acaulis*. Sun and moist, well-drained soil it must have; we have plenty of fresh air at 700 feet, but beyond that nobody has as yet fathomed its secret cravings so as to make it bloom with the abandon that it is minded to do in some places. Some species appear to flower more freely than others; one of which we have experience is *G. clusii* but, then on moving it to this garden, it has been less free! On the other hand, *G. alpina*, a small plant which has almost stemless flowers, rarely fails to flower from the smallest piece. However, this grows in the rock garden, its only seeming fads being extra good drainage and lime-free soil. It was raised from seed from an original free flowering plant, flowering in its third year. Sometimes it would seem that the new life (seed raised) must have an advantage over the ever-divided and over-divided plant, and this might well be tried with *acaulis*.

Other first favourites of those excitements of the spring are *Pulsatilla vulgaris*—rather a derogatory title after knowing them so long under the pleasing name of *Anemone pulsatilla*. These capture the hardest of hearts and the untutored eye of even non-gardeners, so lavish are they with their lovely large, silky golden-centred cups. Though pulsatillas like their lime, we have never found them less free flowering in neutral or acid soil, but they do pay for good dressings of bonemeal in such soils. Once planted, they should be left alone and not moved, for from then onwards, each year will bring forth the joy of more and more flowers from their increasing crowns. They are long-lived plants, how long we do not know, for when we have had to move garden, 10–12-year-old plants have been growing even better and better, and still giving dozens of blossoms.

After flowering, pulsatillas extend their ferny, carroty leaves, but then pass into another period of beauty with lovely silken seed heads. Seeds are the best means of increasing them, and these should be sown as soon as they are ripe, and then they will come up in a few weeks. With care, these will flower in their second or third year. The type plant varies from mauve to imperial purple, lovely in any shade, but whites, pinks, reds, and the darkest of violet in *P. mallanderi*, can all contribute to the beauty of herbaceous borders and the sunny sides of shrub borders. Choosing plants at nurseries can be thrilling, and a variety of forms may be chosen, besides such cultivars as 'Mrs Van der Elst', pink; 'White Swan' a very good white; *rubra*, reddish-brown, and other red shades. One of the most enchanting and rather rare is P. 'Budapest', pale lavender-blue. The other glorious pulsatillas, *alpina*, and 'Sulphurea' are for the faster drainage of the rock garden or exceptionally well-drained border, the former having huge white flowers, and the latter golden yellow.

Greater use can be made of some of the dwarf phlox for borders, and as these succeed the pulsatillas in flower, they may well be grown alongside, as long as the pulsatillas have their allotted 12-inches space. Such species as *Phlox ovata*, *P. pilosa* and some of the stronger growing varieties of *P. subulata* such as 'Fairy', 'Temiscaming', the old 'G. F. Wilson' and others, also make fine low evergreen carpets to accentuate the form and outline of shrubs.

Phlox ovata is an easily grown species with showy heads of inch-wide, rose-pink flowers on foot-high stems in May, and often again later. It forms a low tuft of evergreen leaves, not unlike *P. divaricata* (syn. *P. canadensis*), another North American semi-woodland plant which will also do well away from the fullest sun. The latter carries large heads of lavender-blue flowers on erect 8-inch stems in May. *P. pilosa*, very close to the latter in general habit, is also erect, bearing clusters of rose-pink flowers on foot-high stems.

For later flowering, a little species of aster from Kashmir, *Aster thomsonii* 'Nana', a neat clump-forming plant, requires the minimum of attention and is happy enough in full sunshine. We like this as there are never too many flowers out at one time. That may be a personal taste, but in some cases we prefer to see the beauty of each single flower rather than in a mass, where perhaps one cannot see 'the wood for the trees'. It is graceful in a refined way with enough flowers out at once for it to be effective. Starting in late July, with inch-wide flowers of pale lavender-blue on thin erect stems of 10–12 inches, it carries on till autumn, being a good complementary plant to *Polygonum vacciniifolium*.

The taller sedums are among those in Chapter 2, Favourite Herbaceous Perennials, but the forms of *Sedum spectabile* with their colourful heads, can also be used in the foreground to break up any tendency to uniformity in height when there are too many low-growing plants. However, *S.* 'Ruby Glow', an Award of Merit plant, which is a hybrid between *S.* 'Autumn Joy' and the small rock garden plant *S. cauticola*, is a most colourful dwarf which rarely exceeds 6–8 inches and sprawls forward with up-turned heads. It forms an attractive glaucous-leaved clump, from which the flower stems give 5–6 inch wide heads of ruby-red in the later days of August and into September. It is very free flowering and most aptly named, and also a good grower.

The stokesias go well alongside the latter, *Stokesia laevis* 'Praecox' beginning in August and still being in flower with the sedums. It is a North American known as Stoke's aster, and it is characterized by an evergreen basal clump of dark leathery leaves and 3-inch wide flowers of soft lavender-blue on 6–8-inch stems. The white cultivar, and 'Blue Moon' pale blue, are good alternatives for blending in with other plants, and also mix well around roses. They are free flowering, easily grown in full sunshine, carry on from year to year, and may be divided in spring so as to enlarge the planting.

Two potentillas, generally known as rock garden plants, *Potentilla tridentata* and *P. alba*, are most useful low, space-fillers which behave well in the ordinary border. Not only does *P. alba* brighten winter days with a ground hugging mat of silvery-edged fresh green leaves, but scarcely misses a month without a flower or two. Late April to May is its main season of blossom, when it is studded with pure white strawberry-like flowers, sitting close upon the foliage; these are solid little ¾-inch wide, golden-centred flowers of quality. *P. alba* gives a foot wide clump and more, and though never overbearing in its claim to territory, a few together can be close cover to exclude weeds, and it will accommodate itself to partly shady places. *P. tridentata*, having rather quickly outgrown its allotted rock garden space, was moved into our sand bed, not in disgrace, for it has a dainty charm, but to make room for other arrivals. Here it proved a perfect dwarf ground-coverer, no wit distressed by poor fare. It is yet another evergreen for furnishing, and though it spreads well, it keeps neat and compact and has small glossy leaves. In May it sends out elegant little white flowers a few inches above the tuft. In all it will cover some 18 inches of space.

Potentilla megalantha can claim a place with these prostrate ones, for it is handsome enough in its leafage of silvery-velvet. May and June sees its large golden, short stemmed strawberry-like flowers. *P. erecta* 'Warrensii' which had an Award of Merit many years ago, has always moved with us, generally from its self-sown seedlings which always come true to type. It is one of those with taller branching flower sprays, up to 15–18 inches, with large, clear yellow blossoms. Starting in May, there is hardly a month when a few flowers are not out. There is no lack of colour among these taller ones, for instance *P. argyrophylla* 'Atrosanguinea' having large florin-sized dark red flowers, and handsome silvery leaves. The old 'Gibson's Scarlet', dazzling scarlet, still holds its place as one of the most effective, and as well as doubles and other shades, 'Yellow Queen' is a good choice. They need planting in groups to be fully effective.

For sunny positions the campanula family gives us the platy-codons, known as the balloon flowers, for as their flower buds gradually swell they look like shining balloons. When they finally open, their powder-blue campanula-like bells are almost 3 inches across. In *Platycodon grandiflorus* the flowers are amply supported on glaucous-leaved stems of 2 feet or more, and if grown in the open in full sun, usually hold themselves up well. *P. grandiflorus mariesii*, and the white form, are a little over a foot in height, have equally bold flowers, and are very often grown in the rock garden.

These Japanese balloon flowers have been grown in this country for almost 200 years, and are one of the most useful of later summer flowers. Again, they are well worth generous grouping, and may be close-planted, for their fleshy non-spreading roots take up very little room. They die away in autumn and do not appear again until May, and are also easily grown. Apart from marking their place, they may safely be left to their own devices to come up year after year. Coming easily and well from seed, they soon reach flowering size. There is an even smaller form of 8–10 inches, *P. grandiflorus* 'Apoyama', also with very large flowers. It is perfect for the rock garden or miniature border and is proving just as trustworthy.

With the influx of so many new and good plants, too often we forget the trusty old ones such as our native *Campanula glomerata* in its best form, *C. glomerata dahurica*, or *C. g.* 'Superba' with close heads of royal purple. At 1–1½ feet it is one of the best of the short border plants, and forms a good spread in almost any soil. Though white forms are catalogued at times, it is a wonder that other shades have not been developed, for on Salisbury Plain during the Second War, I found pale lavender and good pink forms on the Downland. Having duly marked them for collection, of course we moved off the very next day!

Having been in cultivation so long, *C. carpatica* from the Carpathians has waxed prosperous in our land and furnished a sturdy race of children which are just as easy, vigorous and invaluable as edges for borders and rose beds. *C. carpatica* makes hearty clumps and rises to 6–8 inches, producing large open flattish cups of mauve or white from June onwards. As for her offspring, nobody can go far wrong in planting 'Convexity', 'Isobel', 'Riverslea', 'White Star' and other lovely named ones.

Campanula poscharskyana gives good value for its name, sending out far-reaching, low, trailing and climbing sprays of pale lavender-blue, starry flowers. It is very floriferous and showy, but should be used with care, perhaps on corners where it can be curbed, or in rough places or awkward endings which such ground coverings may transform to loveliness.

Our own native harebell, *C. rotundifolia*, with its pretty pale blue bells in mid-summer, is also worthy of its place round border edges as well as its usual place in the rock garden. On the whole the campanula family is relished by slugs, but *rotundifolia* seems immune and is also a good permanent doer. A pygmy form of the tall *C. lactiflora* is *C. l.* 'Pouffe', which is ideal for the foreground and forms a neat mound about 9–10 inches high and gives a free display of pale lavender-blue flowers from June onwards.

In amongst the smaller tufted plants the spiky growers have their architectural value and give distinction and contrast. The big verbascums, tall and stately, play their role in the background, but for the foreground *V. phoeniceum* rarely exceeds 18 inches and is a pretty species. It bears slender flower spikes of violet-purple, but is variable from seed and can be rose, lilac or white and other shades. It needs well drained positions to survive more than a few seasons but comes quickly from seed and will also sow itself.

Blue is always a favourite colour and especially anything approaching gentian blue. One of the hound's tongues, *Cynoglossum nervosum*, fulfills this desire with showers of intense deep blue, forget-me-not flowers on slender waving branches for many weeks from late May till July. It is an elegant little plant with a backing of narrow dark green leaves to its 15–18-inch height. Despite coming from the Himalayas, like a large number of the beauties that come from there, it turns out to be a good perennial in any ordinary soil. Several together are most effective and this is easily accomplished by raising it from seed.

Some of the lychnis are useful tufty plants for edging borders, our own native *Lychnis viscaria* taking up little room with its dark grassy clump. Maybe its rosy-crimson heads are a strong colour, but then most of the pink family usually supply the high tones. Its double cultivar *L. viscaria* 'Splendens Plena' is even brighter in a fierce carmine pink, but these can be matched and blended with the smaller, grey-foliaged edgers such as the later flowering dianthus, *Stachys lanata* or *Veronica cinerea*.

For the later summer flowering and behind the lychnis, the dwarf *Buphthalmum salicifolium* is a choice plant of 18 inches. Though this is an alpine meadow plant of Europe, it is easily grown in any sunny border and one plant can soon be divided to make a group. It is very surprising that it is not used more, for its 2-inch wide, yellow daisy flower heads are most cheerful and stand up well to wind and rain.

The astilbes should really be included among the moisture lovers or those for boggy soil but are very useful in the foreground where a border may face away from the sun and be fairly moist; part shade from shrubs or other plants can be a helpful factor. Those who want some colour in late July, August and into September, will find *Astilbe simplicifolia*, *A. chinensis pumila* and *A. crispa* most valuable, especially for limited spaces. *A. simplicifolia* from Japan, is the daintiest of dwarfs, its spires of creamy, feathery plumes held over ferny foliage, and no more than 6–8 inches high. There is also *A. simplicifolia* 'Rosea', a little taller and of a delicate rose-pink. The pygmy, *A. chinensis pumila*, keeps its crinkly foliage close to the ground and sends up fascinating erect, fluffy plumes of 10–12 inches in pinky-crimson; several together are very effective. *A.* × *crispa* is one of the 'Tom Thumbs' which gives an exciting mat of ground-hugging, crinkled, finely cut leaves in late spring. This fascinating dark leafage lives up to one's expectations of something good, and in the late summer it raises 6-inch, stiff, erect pyramids with short branching sprays of pink flowers. We have only had the type plant, but there are a few named ones to be searched for, such as 'Perkeo'. Another doll's house one is *A. glaberrima* 'Saxatilis', again from the treasure house of Japan; this is a mere 3–4 inches in height, with sprays of dainty pink flowers. It is a plant to be cherished among other specials for intimate shady places.

In the sunshine and for the foreground of the herbaceous border or shrub border there are a number of low growing hardy geraniums, compact growers that all help to exclude weeds. A chosen favourite that immediately springs to mind is *Geranium renardii*, not so much for any show of flowers as for its singular, even dome of velvety, grey-green leaves. Making a dense clump from a woody rootstock, its rounded leaf-shape is perfectly lobed, and above these are carried quite large French grey flowers, lightly veined in purple. An unusual colour though not perhaps exciting to some, but as easily placed as its lovely foliage. Yet another attractive foliage species is *G. macrorrhizum*, a more vigorous spreader, especially suitable where ground-cover is a consideration. Spreading low upon the ground, it may be used in sun or among shrubs in part shade where it will flower just as freely. One of its joys is its aromatic foliage, and then, in June, the pale pink flowers stand erect upon the greenery.

Among these dwarf summer flowering species we would never like to be without two of our native plants, *G. sanguineum* and *G. s. lancastriense*. The former, the bloody cranesbill, with blood red to crimson-purple flowers, may not be to all tastes but it merges in with silver-leaved plants. Whether or no its colour may appeal, it is very free flowering, and numerous forms abound which can be more pleasing; in *sanguineum* 'Album' on the other hand, we have a really graceful plant. With more delicately cut foliage, this is a stronger grower with a long succession of glistening white flowers. *G. s. lancastriense* is dwarfer than *sanguineum*, always adorable, whether in the rock garden or in full sun at the border edge. It has large, wide open, soft pink flowers, delicately veined, and these hover over the mat of finely divided greenery for a very long season.

A most useful plant for mixing in, and one that is too rarely seen, is *G. aconitifolium*, which is mid-way between the smaller ones and the larger growers. It is one of the earliest of the geraniums to flower, its pure white, funnel-shaped blooms, coming along in May when some of the flaunting colours of the tulip species may need a little light relief.

Most notable of these herbaceous geraniums for long flowering is *G. grandiflorum alpinum* with clusters of wide-open cups of a rich blue. It is a strong grower, forming a low dense colony that fills a space where weeds might be. Here and there in the garden, flowering almost throughout the season are *G. endressii*, and its varieties 'Rose Clair' and 'A. T. Johnson' which give a welcome range of colour in clear rose, rosy-pink and silvery-pink; they are easy going and are tolerant of some shade, and are in the 12–15-inch range of height. A much later acquisition, and by no means to be overlooked by lovers of geraniums, is the species *nodosum*. Only now and then does one come upon this, but its cool lilac flowers are unusual and are borne over much of the summer from a low clump of bright, dark green, shiny leaves.

In quite a different category are the clump forming lathyrus. These neat little plants of the pea family tend to be rather neglected, yet they are the earliest of herbaceous plants to flower and are valuable for the very front of the border, rock garden or margins of woodland. Only *Lathyrus cyaneus* (syn. *Orobus cyaneus*) and *L. aurantiacus* have so far come our way but, so thrifty and everlasting are they, that others must be worth the seeking. The bushy growth and fresh green leaves of *L. cyaneus* hardly reach a foot and in early spring it is smothered with little pea flowers of bright blue. The pretty *L. aurantiacus* is equally modest in its territorial claims, scarcely exceeding a foot across and greeting the spring with flowers of an unusual tawny orange-yellow.

An unusual plant to grow in the midget border or mixed in with the front-row furnishing is our own adorable *Potentilla rupestris.* It is a rare plant now, and even as scarce in nurserymen's lists, but it is also a plant that is by no means amiss in the best of rock gardens. Its flowers are dainty, elegant and graceful as any plant needs to be for inclusion among the best. Rising to a mere 15–18 inches, it greets the lengthening days of spring with pure white, inch-wide, open flowers, all the more charming for their clusters of golden stamens. Over and above its fresh greenery, its branching stems maintain the display for many weeks. Unlike some of the potentillas it has desirable compactness of form, as well as a constitution that would regard the suggestion of any rich feeding as a piece of insolence.

Calamintha nepetoides also has this desirable quality of compactness of form, though it might not be a plant to impress all visitors. Besides embodying grace and elegance in its continuous outbreak of tiny thimbles of pale lavender coloured flowers from July onwards, it fulfills our requirements in looking after itself. Though small, the mass of flowers, standing up on 12-inch stems, is notably effective at a distance and the bees delight in its nectar.

Where there is a fancy for a startling patch of colour, *Lychnis* x *haageana* is first rate if the soil is fairly moist and well drained. Barely exceeding a foot in height, it is topped by brilliant orange-red, catherine-wheel shaped flowers 2 inches wide which glow above dark green foliage. As it is easily raised from seed with but little variation in colour, it is inexpensive to get a massed effect; plants will bloom in the second season. It is well placed alongside the silvery-grey of *Anaphalis triplinervis* and is not averse to the part shade that the latter enjoys.

A small rock garden or front-of-the-border plant which is not often seen is *Inula ensifolia*. It has a quiet appeal, a small tuffet-forming plant that sends up large, golden-rayed daisy flowers in early August. Its dwarf habit entitles it to a place with the low growers in sun and light soil. An occasional division seems to give it new vigour.

In the same category is *Linum flavum*, one of the few yellows in this family. In the early spring yellow seems a predominant colour, but later in the summer it is in more short supply, so that this linum with its ample, open and glowing golden-yellow blooms is very welcome. The habit, too, is so correct, no flopping but nicely erect with the flowers borne on short branching stems in June, and even on into August. It is a good perennial in well-drained sunny places.

The prunellas also maintain a good evergreen appearance and are well suited to give colourful drifts for edging or paving pockets. They are much improved versions of our own native self-heal, *Prunella vulgaris*, and colour forms give a range of reddish, rose, blue and white. Besides flowering very freely and growing into close clumps, their value lies in summer and autumn flowering. Their short stumpy spikes of a few inches carry rounded heads of flowers. One of the best of them and most generally grown is *P.* 'Loveliness' with good heads of clear lavender flowers. Then there is *P. grandiflora*, strong growing with heads of rich blue, *P. incisa* with reddish-purple flowers, and *P. webbiana* with taller spikes of rosy-purple. They are not particular about soil but, like most of the labiates, enjoy sun and warmth.

A first-rate contrast to the dark foliage of the latter and of the same family, is the golden form of the common marjoram, *Origanum vulgare* 'Aurea'. It forms a neat little bush of 6 inches high, serving as a dense foot-wide covering for the soil. In the spring its small leaves are bright gold, the colour being maintained through the year.

The dianthus family must not be forgotten among the sun-lovers and plants for edging borders and also for the rock garden. To embark on a description of all of them and their individual merits would fill a small book. They are of the highest garden value and as much a backbone of colour as the roses, irises, phlox and many other large families in their turn. We always look forward to 'dianthus time', in May and June and even later, when their delicious fragrance fills the evening air. With very few exceptions they are sun-lovers, and do best in the lightest soil. However, as regards lime, we have always gardened on neutral or acid soil and find that they grow and flower well enough without it, especially if given plenty of bonemeal. The named forms of pinks, rock garden hybrids and species are almost legion, and so we leave the choice to our readers. Yet while on the subject of these, the much-loved Sweet William of old cottage gardens is indispensable in any border and its scent is unsurpassed.

✻ 4 ✻

The Evergreen Woodlanders

WHILE HEADING this 'The Evergreen Woodlanders', let none
be discouraged, for it does not necessarily mean that to grow these,
one must have a natural woodland. The presence of a few taller
shrubs and evergreen specimens are enough to create the conditions of a thin woodland of light shade. A glade can be an
attractive feature in the smallest of gardens, and using viburnums,
cornus, cotoneasters, ornamental cherries and so on will give
walks through partly shaded borders. Very often the neighbouring trees, which may give shade in the small garden, can often be
turned to good account, and shade lovers be grown where perhaps nothing would thrive before. There are many lovely plants
for shady positions, but the majority of them die down for the
winter. To have some semblance of life in these shady borders, it
is desirable to have a smattering of evergreens and often these
produce a good turn of colour at the onset of winter.

Some of the handsome foliaged bergenias assume this change
with tones of red in early autumn, and remain so until the spring.
Now the values of foliage and weed suppressing are more
esteemed, these good old garden plants have deservedly come into
favour again. While they grow in any soil in sun or shade, they
flower better where the sun will reach them at some time of the
day. Their great leaves are broad and luxuriant all the year, making
wonderful patches of ground covering edging which has to us
been especially useful in smothering sorrel, one of our worst
weeds. They are also an excellent contrast to grassy-leaved plants
and erect growers that may flower at a later date, such as *Aster
divaricatus* (syn. *A. corymbosus*), and they are a good foil to deciduous

shrubs in winter time. Like most of their cousins the saxifrages, they bloom in the spring and have strong, erect 10–15-inch flower spikes with massive heads. The individual flowers which are large, may be white, pink, rose or red and last very well when cut for the house. There are numerous species and an increasing number of good coloured hybrids. There is a great variety in size of leaf and edging of the leaves, from heart-shaped to rounded or great spoon-shaped ones; the largest of the evergreen species are *cordifolia* and *crassifolia*. *B. delavayi* is particularly rich in the colouring of its dark red flowers, and is most ornamental in winter time when the leaves have changed to an even plum-purple, remaining so until late spring when they revert to green again. *B. ciliata* is not always reliably evergreen and should be grown in more shelter. Its large hairy leaves are very lovely, and its graceful sprays of greeny-white flowers appear in March.

Though it is deciduous, we must mention among these *B. afghanica* which is a smaller foliaged and neat plant, flowering in March before the leaves come out. The flowers are pure white tinged with pink. The following are evergreen: *B.* 'Delbees', 'Silberlicht' (Silverlight) and 'Abendglut', and are among the good hybrids which can now be obtained.

The once popular London Pride, *Saxifraga umbrosa*, can again take its place as a useful labour saver, for its large, evergreen, close-growing rosettes give little room for weeds. It delights in cool shady edges, giving a drift of hazy pink in May with its dainty sprays of flower. For the collector of unusual variants, there is *S. umbrosa* 'Variegata' with handsome variegation of gold, white and green. Though mentioned here, it should have some sun and also poor soil to retain its best colour. There are other smaller forms of the *umbrosa* section of these saxifrages which also do well in shade. Among these are *S. umbrosa* 'Primuloides', a miniature London Pride, a dear little plant that forms tight colonies of small, dark green rosettes and fairy spires of pink flowers. As neat, and even smaller, is *S.u. primuloides* 'Ingwersen's Variety', with dark red flowers. These miniatures form foot-wide patches which are ideal for carpeting intimate shady corners or small borders, but require well-drained soil. Yet another, but stronger growing is *S. umbrosa* 'Melvillei', as hearty in its growth as London pride but differing in its smaller and more interesting rosettes.

The Mossy saxifrages also appreciate these cooler, partially shaded walks, and give wide, low carpets of mossy emerald green for the path edge. In April and May their green carpets are dotted over with graceful sprays of flowers varying in height from 3–6 inches, in whites, pinks, and every shade of red. Such aristocratic names as 'Pearly King', 'Crimson King', 'Pompadour', down to such fairies as 'Peter Pan' and 'Pixie', are among the many named ones that are supplied.

Also of this family are the tiarellas, woodland plants of North America which are perfectly at home in our shady places. We have always loved *Tiarella cordifolia* with its spires of creamy foam, like some miniature spiraea. It can be most effective as a wave of cream, massed and under carpeting shrubs or marching along a shady streamside. Its clumps of vine-like leaves, flat upon the ground, are always delightful in their changing hues, assuming bronzy and pink tints and then returning to normal pale green when the fresh leaves break again in the spring. It spreads by a network of runners, and blooms in May or June. *T. trifoliata* is less common, a very desirable and charming plant that differs in remaining in a self contained clump, slowly increasing to some 6 inches or so across; it is one that will satisfy the tidy minded gardener. In a shady spot and good soil, it puts up 12–15-inch heuchera-like spikes of bloom with airy, silvery-white bells from summer till very late autumn. For the collector who cares for the dainty treasures, there is *T. polyphylla* to add to these, a hardy, slow growing and compact species which bears small creamy-white flowers and has a good turn of colour for the winter.

Yet another of this vast saxifrage family is the clump-forming *Tellima grandiflora* whose evergreen leaves will cover wide patches of the wilder parts of the woodland and shady ends of the border. An autumn turn of colour to these large, green, heuchera-like leaves is intensified by the onslaught of winter. It will be appreciated by those who can admire nature's more delicate and subtle works in greenish and yellow shaded flowers. In May it sends up numerous slim, 18-inch spires from which are poised a profusion of well-spaced fringed bells of greenish-white. Their grace and beauty can best be admired when the sun glints upon them through a woodland glade.

Cardamine trifolia, one of the *Cruciferae*, is of the lesser carpeters, a dainty treasure in its own right, which may be associated with other choice plants of cool favourite places or a north border by the house where special treasures may be assembled. Forming low, close evergreen mats of very dark, shiny trefoil leaves, it steadily weaves a tidy 12–15-inch clump that can be a pleasure in the smallest winter garden. Then, in March and April, just when we are looking for a miracle and a little encouragement, *C. trifolia* sends up its 5–6-inch stems of showy white flowers to cheer these early days.

In all our gardens *Galax aphylla* has been one of the chosen ones, and we have rejoiced in its big bonny, shining leafage. We regard it as one of the most handsome of the woodland evergreens, for it is always beautiful to look upon in winter time and has a sufficient turn of colour to be even more attractive with tints of bronze and red. It forms hearty clumps of dark green upstanding, rounded 3-inch wide leaves, and creeps slowly at the root, but in compactness, making one of the best of ground covering woodlanders. It is at its best in moist shade and almost sunless places, where its narrowly tapering spires of white flowers show up clearly and to best effect. It is in early June that this closely set inflorescence is pushed up over the foliage to stand 15–18 inches above it.

The shortias are easily the next best in the matter of ornamental foliage, and these are also lovers of shade, and are true woodland plants that come from Japan as well as from the same regions as the galax. All are dwarf plants which form close, evergreen tufts of glossy green leaves. In the autumn they assume striking shades of reddish-bronze, more so if the soil is moist enough to permit their being grown in some sunshine. Not only is their foliage so satisfactory to look upon, and especially if they spread to foot-wide patches, but the sheer beauty and delicacy of their flowers is enthralling. *Shortia galacifolia* comes from North America and is often classed as a shrub, increasing itself very slowly by short stoloniferous growths. It blooms in early spring, the stems rising through the foliage to 4–6 inches, on which the inch-wide flowers are borne; these are very lovely, blush-white, bell-shaped and delicately frilled at the edges, and are usually carried singly. *S. uniflora*, from Japan, is even more entrancing with larger, more open flowers of white to pale pink, but even surpassing this is *S. uniflora* 'Grandiflora' with yet larger, 2-inch wide, frilly blossoms of a delicate shade of soft pink. These Japanese species are more compact growing, with leaves larger than *galacifolia*, and more rounded and polished; they take on gorgeous shades of red and crimson in the autumn. They are all perfectly hardy, but demand lime-free soil and careful cultivation with plenty of leaf-mould, peat and coarse sand to make the soil friable and well drained. A position where it is always reasonably moist suits them best, and some of the finest patches we have seen have been on the north border of a house wall, at least 25–30 years old and still spreading quite happily.

Belonging to the same family (*Diapensiaceae*) and requiring the same care in cultivation but tolerant of a little more sun are the schizocodons. With bronzy-red shiny leaves, so beautiful in winter time, it is enough to say that even disinterested non-gardeners have remarked: 'Oh what colour, how delightful!' Japan gives us *Schizocodon soldanelloides* and *S. s. magnus*, which are more compact and smaller leaved than the shortias, and have leaves close to the ground—the latter larger in leaf. Both have the most entrancing fringed bells of pink, and are held up on 3–4-inch stems in May.

The hellebores hold the unique position of being among the few herbaceous plants that flower during the winter months. In this they are supreme in the size and substance of their flowers and with such a grace of carriage, some bold and erect, others modestly nodding. Their hardiness is amazing, often being bowed down by overnight frost, yet with the easier temperature of the later part of the day, they soon stand erect again and totally undamaged, without even any difference to the setting of their seed. They are best in partially shaded places, shaded and sheltered by shrubs, or in the shade of north walls near the house where winter flowers can be fully appreciated.

Besides *Helleborus niger*, the well-known Christmas rose, there are various species and hybrids which extend the flowering season right into May—a good enough performance for any family of plants. The flowers of all of them have an enchanting quality and a great variety in the form of their nodding cup-shaped blossoms, but all of them so solid, waxen and sumptuous in texture. Their flowers may lack purity of colour, for they are mostly muted shades, the whites and creams being overlaid with greenish tints and the crimson and plum to almost black, are misty, mysterious and sombre, but this all adds to their curious and fascinating charm.

Though mentioned here, *H. niger* is not evergreen, but it is the earliest of these to come into flower, sometimes before Christmas; there are also varieties of this which do not bloom until February or March. It is indispensable for the winter garden, and even one plant will give many blossoms. One of the best forms of it is *H. n. altifolius*, in which the flower stems rise up strongly to 12–15 inches to display the purest of white flowers. *H.* 'Potters Wheel' is another magnificent selected cultivar which flowers from February to March. The species *H. atrorubens* also very often opens its first flowers by the beginning of December, and when well established, may still be in flower in late February. It has smaller, reddish-purple flowers on foot-high stems, is slower growing and does not remain in leaf very long, dying away completely during the summer. Our native, *H. foetidus*, is a plant of character which makes shrubby, dark evergreen bushes of 1½–2 feet, and is outstanding as a small specimen plant. It flowers at the ends of the stems, bearing panicles of pale green, bell-shaped flowers edged with a purple margin. For spring flowering this is unusual and striking and it lasts a long time in flower.

Helleborus argutifolius, now *H. lividus* 'Corsicus', is one of the finest, an ornamental and architectural plant, handsome in its bushy, sub-shrubby habit with bold evergreen foliage. When at its full 2½–3 feet it is an imposing and striking picture with its thick shrubby stems and glaucous foliage. In the spring its large, pale green, 2-inch wide, cup-shaped flowers are formed in great loose heads. For their decorative value, both *foetidus* and *lividus* 'Corsicus' should be grown as isolated specimens. They show up well against darker foliaged shrubs, and these help to protect them against strong winds which are apt to wrench and break them when heavy with blossoms.

We find those known as the Lenten roses (*H. orientalis*), some of the most fascinating and beautiful of all. They are a race of hybrids which are more generally easy of cultivation than any of the others. They have a very wide colour range from white, cream, greeny-whites, many flushed with rose, to dark plum and almost black tones often spotted and freckled within the blooms. In positions round the shady side of the house walls where they can be readily enjoyed in the worst of weather, they will flower from February to April, standing up sturdily to 15–18 inches.

Helleborus kochii has been with us for years, moved and re-sown to bloom again, for they all come readily from seed if it is sown as soon as it is ripe. *Kochii* is considered to be the original *H. orientalis* and is a good grower with almost permanently ever-green foliage and blossoms of an alluring greeny-yellow. On the whole, these hellebores like shade and a fairly rich soil with some lime, but though ours is generally lean and lacking lime, plenty of leafmould and annual dressings of manure keep them thrifty and rewarding. Liking shade, they fit in to the woodland garden well and look very much at home among the shrubs or under trees where it is not too rooty.

Mostly the members of the cornus family are medium and tall shrubs, but an exception is *Cornus canadensis*, a baby dogwood of a few inches. Strictly speaking it is generally regarded as a shrub, but it is one of the most accommodating of carpeters, especially where the soil is lime-free, cool and moist. In Canada it carpets the floor of the woods, and here it is happy enough in such a set-ting, creating perfect ground covering among trees and peeping out from the shady side of shrubs or rhododendrons. Its creeping growths form a colony of large dark green leaves for the summer time, but with the cool of the autumn days or the first frosty weather, they turn a rich pinky tinge. As with many of these cornus, the small flower is surrounded by a large bract, giving the effect of an exceptionally large flower. In *C. canadensis* these are inch-wide, and are a lovely creamy-white, gleaming out from the clump in May and on and off through the summer. When well suited it will form wide running carpets, but its passion for terri-tory excludes it from the company of any choice herbaceous plants.

An old plant which is content enough in shady places, and a good subject for the shady house border is *Francoa ramosa*, appropriately known as bridal wreath. A one-time favourite of cottage gardens, window-boxes and as a greenhouse pot plant, it is rarely seen in gardens now. A member of the saxifrage family, it comes from Chile, and authors of the older gardening books repeatedly refer to it as tender or on the borderline, but plants from our own seed, raised many years ago, are still going strong after having suffered all manner of winters. It is a compact, clump-forming plant with distinct evergreen, lobed, roughish leaves of some 4–6 inches in length. In July and August it produces a number of elegant sprays of 2–2½-foot flower stems with many closely packed white flowers. Because of its reputed tenderness we have usually grown it in sheltered, shady places, but it will also do very well in the sun where it is not too dry. Apart from a small difference in foliage and racemes of blush-pink flowers, *F. sonchifolia* is an equally graceful plant and every bit as hardy.

Also long cultivated in our gardens, and among the most charming of spring flowers are the hepaticas. They come from the woodlands of the Alps and many other places in Europe, and love such cool and shady nooks in the garden. Very often putting up their first flowers in the late winter days of February, their best efforts are reserved for May when they unfold a long succession of ½-inch wide, cup-shaped anemone blossoms varying in colour from blue, violet-blue to pink and white, on 3–4-inch stems. Left alone in rich, well-drained soil, hepaticas form long-lived clumps, satisfying in their glossy, leathery, dark greenery. Hepaticas are often found under *Anemone*, for instance *Hepatica triloba* may be *Anemone hepatica*, and *transsilvanica* may be *Anemone angulosa*, the latter being larger and finer in foliage, and often so in flower, but the older name of hepatica is taking precedence again. At one time, named and double forms were more plentiful, but as fine as the latter are, none seem more lovely than the singles. It is great fun hunting out all manner of different shades, but to get a goodly stock, they are readily raised from seed, which forms quickly and should be taken just at a stage when they come away easily at the touch; if sown immediately they will germinate the following spring. They abhor disturbance and any dividing should be done as soon as they have flowered. *Helonias bullata* from North America, belonging to the lily family, is of value to us for a pleasing and handsome rosette of evergreen foliage. It is dark green and keeps low upon the ground, enjoying any damp, part shady position to the foreground where it will slowly produce more tightly clustered shiny rosettes to play their small part in an all-the-year furnishing scheme. From April to May it produces sturdy 10–12-inch spikes which terminate in a fluff of starry pink flowers. It is suggestive of some rare orchid species and may be regarded as a collector's piece more than a plant which will light up the garden, but it plays its part and will be appreciated by those who like the curiously attractive.

In intimate places and odd corners the value of these evergreens is inestimable for the winter months, and just such another is *Reineckia carnea* from China and Japan. It also belongs to the lily family and is easily grown in a similar cool situation, though not needing so much moisture as helonias seems to thrive upon. Its distinction lies in its low grassy tuft, with broad leaves, some 6 inches long, tapering to a point and arching over gracefully almost in a semi-circle. Increasing slowly by creeping rhizomes, it gradually forms an engaging little clump, from which erect 9-inch flowering spikes arise in April to bear an inflorescence of fragrant pink flowers.

Another of these lesser evergreens is the carpeting *Tanakaea radicans* from the woodlands of Japan. It is unperturbed by winter's onslaughts, evergreen on nature's canvas and displaying a mat of deep green, leathery, serrated leaves which show up flat upon the ground. In early summer little creamy-white sprays of spiraea-like blooms thrust forth from among the foliage. It is a charming treasure that prospers in cool peaty soil, slowly increasing by little runners.

From New Zealand and other Antarctic regions we have a fascinating little fern named *Blechnum penna marina* which does a grand job of ground covering and at the same time is attractive to look at. Forming a low wide carpet only a few inches high, the small fronds are dark green, but its finest hour is in May, for when the new growth appears the whole is transformed to a haze of pinky-bronze. Being perfectly hardy it is ideal for smothering weeds in shady woodland where it will cover square feet, but it is too invasive to grow alongside smaller plants.

Omphalodes cappadocica we hold very dear for its exquisite vivid blue forget-me-not flowers which delight us for many weeks from March onwards, and again in the autumn. Its other assets are its fine evergreen foliage, close growing with pale green, oval pointed leaves, and its hearty way of covering the ground at border edges. Though it is quite happy in moist shade or half-shade, as long as the soil is reasonably moist it will thrive in sun, and makes a good carpeter amidst roses, increasing itself by self-sown seedlings as well.

If you have a fondness for the more humble treasures, one of the daintiest of all evergreen woodlanders is *Linnaea borealis* which is a real forest dweller from northern regions and also a very rare British native. It weaves a prostrate carpet of creeping branches which are clothed with pairs of small rounded, shiny leaves which turn a bronzy tint in winter time. The pairs of dainty, almond-scented, flush-pink bells are enchanting and dangle on thread-like stems of a few inches. If one can imagine and imitate the texture of the forest floor, made up of loose, peaty leafmould, always cool and moist, linnaea should take to this and go ahead rapidly. Sometimes these conditions can best be found in shady pockets of the rock garden where the delights of linnaea may be more easily admired. The form *L. borealis americana* is said to be easier and stronger growing.

Primulas are discussed under 'Other Plants for Shade and Part Shade', page 99, as the majority of them wisely sleep for the winter months. Not so *Primula helodoxa*, for she is thirsty at all times, and will do overtime and be quite happy in boggy places. It is a pleasure to see a group of these primulas in winter, carpeting the ground with large fresh green leaves; there need be no anxiety here as to whether they will ever appear again after all nature's trials of the winter months. The 'glory of the marsh' as this Chinese primula is known, lives up to its name as one of the best. By mid-May, even at 6 inches it starts to show its first tier of golden-yellow flowers, and from thence tier upon tier continues till July when it has reached almost 3 feet. It is easily raised from seed and if well cared for will flower the following year. These moisture-loving primulas are very rewarding when raised from seed, nearly all flowering the next season. The entrancing *P. secundiflora* with reddish-purple flowers in June, is another that generally remains evergreen.

Whilst *Wulfenia carinthiaca* may not be a true woodlander it has the virtue of interesting, shiny, evergreen rosettes of crinkled leaves which lie flat upon the ground. As far as we are concerned it fits into our idea of doing some splendid winter furnishing. As it likes a cool root run, it is always happy somewhere in the shade and is quite a useful one to add to those 'special edgers' for the north side of the house. Mostly it produces its 9-inch spikes of deep blue flowers in June and July, but usually adds a few more in the autumn. Then there is *W. amherstiana*, more showy and elegant in its racemes of lilac flowers which are narrow and closely packed to one side of the stem, very much like a small hosta. It differs in its evergreen rosette being crinkled, and it does best where its shady place is extra well drained. *W. baldaccii* is also for choice, north facing places. Smaller in leaf than the others, it has short spikes of dark violet flowers.

Closely related to these wulfenias is the North American synthyris which makes small evergreen clumps. It is a choice, slow-growing plant that is a very good perennial and also enjoys half-shade. In time *Synthyris reniformis* forms clumps of dark green, rather leathery foliage and when well established produces quite a mass of short spikes of bright blue flowers which last for a good month. In flower it is rather like an enlarged milkwort.

Any of these plants are welcome, when their foliage persists to fill the scene for winter enjoyment. Such is our native Gladwyn iris (*Iris foetidissima*), with its handsome sheaf of arching, deep green, sword-shaped leaves. In coastal areas it carpets woods and shady places, often on quite steep slopes, and even on the chalky Sussex Downs. In the garden its creeping rhizomes soon get a foothold in unoccupied shady places round trees and other almost unplantable spaces, often to make a good foil for other plants. Its dull, livid purple flowers in June are maybe of little account, its beauty being in its brilliant orange-red seeds which show from gaping capsules in autumn and deep into the winter. Worth seeking and more pleasing with its pale yellow flowers, is *I. foetidissima* 'Lutea' which also has brilliant seed pods.

Woodland scene. An ideal setting for woodland plants

Galax aphylla. First class among the ground-covering plants

J. R. A. Davies

Astrantia major

Arum creticum

Donald F. Merrett

Boykinia aconitifolia. Doing a job of covering under shrubs

J. R. A. Davies

Roy Elliott

Erythroniums. Massed in woodland setting

Roy Elliott

Roscoea humeana

Lysimachia ciliata. Starting a long season of flower in semi-shade

Erythronium 'White Beauty'

Roy Elliott

J. R. A. Davies

J. R. A. Davies

Melittis melissophyllum

Those who have a shady position and a naturally peaty soil should try some of the aristocratic ourisias. One which grows well for us in a moist pocket where nearby trees provide some shade is *Ourisia macrophylla*, an alpine species from New Zealand. When at rest in winter time, its lush, healthy looking dark green leaves lie flat upon the ground, forming a plantain-like mat. In May it sends up erect flower stalks of 12 inches which terminate in a generous cluster of open-lipped, creamy-white flowers. It creeps along the soil, rooting as it goes and makes a good evergreen cover. *O. coccinea* (syn. *O. elegans*) is also insistent upon shade and moisture and gives wide mats of evergreen foliage. This one comes from Chile and has gorgeous, scarlet tubular flowers over a carpet of bright green leaves. Its flowers are penstemon-like and, like so many Chilean plants, it is really brilliant in its colouring. If suited it will form hearty clumps of crinkled leaves.

If there is a shady position where moisture readily drains away and it faces north or north-east, the evergreen ramondas present satisfactory large-leaved rosettes. They inhabit cliffs of the European Alps and it is usual to plant them in shady rocky crevices, but we find them quite amenable as long as the ground is sloping away from their rosettes. Even then they will appreciate the cool of flat pieces of sandstone rock under their tufts of leaves. They belong to the gloxinia (*Gesneriaceae*) family and have very beautiful clusters of primrose-like flowers of lavender shades with golden stamens, on short flower stems spraying out from the rough leaves in May. They are perfectly hardy and are very long-lived plants. *R. myconii* (syn. *R. pyrenaica*) is the species usually met with, but there are also *R. nathaliae* and *R. serbica*, both very lovely. Sometimes they will remain in one very large rosette, but more often they form a clump of several rosettes.

The haberleas are closely related, but have smoother leaves and form much larger clumps. Their lavender flowers are funnel-shaped, more like those of a miniature gloxinia. Cultivation is the same, except that they will stand much more in the way of sun and are more easily grown. *Haberlea rhodopensis* and *H. ferdinandicoburgii* both have lavender flowers and *H. rhodopensis* 'Virginalis' is a most lovely white form.

Though *Polygala chamaebuxus* and its variety 'Purpurea' are semi-shrubby plants, they can be classed with the best of evergreen woodland carpeters. They inhabit thin alpine woodlands in Central Europe and thrive happily enough in this country, even cheering our early winter months with a few flowers, then their general burst of flower comes in the spring. They spread into very satisfying bright green, foot-wide mats of greenery which are scarcely ever out of flower. The blossoms of *P. chamaebuxus* are little pea flowers of yellow with a cream lip, and are held on short sprays which just peep from amid the foliage. The variety 'Purpurea' has brilliant carmine and yellow flowers.

We are fortunate in having our native hard fern, *Blechnum spicant* established in all manner of places, dry, moist and shady. Its dark evergreen fronds cover steep banks and many an area where it would be difficult to plant anything. But more thought should be given to the handsome *B. tabulare*, for it needs some shelter. In protected bays between shrubs, where it is cool and moist we have never known it come to any harm. Its broad, 2-foot long, evergreen leaves form liberal ground-cover. The fascinating native pygmy fern, *Ceterach officinarum*, the scaly spleenwort, can always be accommodated in shady niches of the rock garden. It is most distinct with its small, blunt, leathery fronds, which are covered with rusty brown felt on the undersides, earning it the title of 'rusty-back'. It is a lime-loving species but growing well in our acid soil, though with the addition of plenty of bonemeal. Sometimes in the summer when it is dry, the fronds roll up to reveal the rusty-brown undersides, but it soon recovers when more humid conditions prevail.

Many an old gardening book leads us to believe that *Saxifraga sarmentosa* (mother of thousands) is not hardy but we have always grown it as a woodland plant and no winter has yet destroyed it. Grown round the base of shrubs, or to form a perfectly flat carpet under rhododendrons or acers, a group of it can form a unique contrast, for its rounded fleshy leaves are so beautifully marked and variegated with silver and red. It belongs to the Diptera group of saxifrages, the same as *S. fortunei* and it carries identical sprays of unevenly petalled flowers.

Euphorbia robbiae is another plant which will flourish at the base of shrubs and in the shade of trees. It can be bracketed with

Hypericum calycinum as one of the finest of dense, low-ground coverers which will fill in round shady walls and even up to hedges. It is a lustrous dark green and, marching on by suckering growths, each closely growing stem will bear an arching crozier of green flowers.

For a really flat-ground coverer the semi-shrubby *Rubus fockeanus* thrusts itself along the ground like ivy, clinging very closely to the ground and rooting as it goes. Unlike the majority of the bramble family it is not armed with spines. It really is an excellent evergreen, for its rounded leaves are large, an unchanging beautiful dark green and notable for being very crinkled. It always seems to be quite happy in any shady position and produces curious little puckered, greenish-white flowers from among the leaves. It is rampageous and should be kept away from smaller plants.

Though we grow the periwinkles (vincas) in shade and half-shade, using them chiefly as ground-cover, they will flower more freely if given fairly sunny positions. They are wonderful evergreens, and can be used in almost any garden for covering under trees, over old tree stumps or almost any barren place, doing this with a hearty willingness and at the same time preventing evaporation from the soil. There is a great variety in their foliage, from glossy dark green to variegated cultivars with silver margined leaves and golden variegation, and the familiar periwinkle flowers include various shades of blue, wine-red and pure white, together with double cultivars of each.

If large areas are to be covered, the varieties of *Vinca major* are the most rampageous, but the cultivars of *V. minor* are neater and include some of the best. *V. minor* 'Bowles' Variety' is one of the finest, quite one of our favourites, free flowering with large, rich violet-blue flowers and large, dark green leaves. *V. m.* 'Argentea Variegata' has pale blue flowers and silver-edged leaves, and *V. m.* 'Variegata' golden variegation and blue flowers. Then there is 'Burgundy' with wine-red flowers, and 'Burgundy Plena', with semi-double, wine-red flowers. Also, there is *V. m.* 'Alba', and *V. m.* 'Alboplena', a white flowered double. All of these frequently send out odd blooms throughout the winter as well as flowering at their best in May and June.

One of the most interesting species is *V. difformis* which is an erect grower and well worth a place near the house, as its large, pale French-grey flowers are produced in November and December, and into May. It grows up to 18 inches and its tangled masses will cover as much space across; it is best cut down after flowering. All these are classed as soft-wooded shrubs, the only true herbaceous one being *V. herbacea* which dies down in winter, coming to life in the spring. It then sends out new slender branches which bear clear blue flowers in the late spring and through the summer; this is really best in the open.

A little carpeter which will form running clumps and an attractive dense mass of evergreen, 3-lobed leaves is *Waldsteinia ternata*. It will thrive in sun or part-shade under trees and is a splendid ground-coverer. No more than a few inches high, it sends up short sprays of golden-yellow, strawberry-like flowers in early summer and spasmodically during the later summer.

The hardy cyclamen make an astonishingly pretty picture when they are planted either in drifts, or have established themselves by the hundred from self-sown seedlings. It is something that will happen if they are planted in semi-woodland which is not disturbed or forked over. They can be planted round old tree stumps, about the boles of trees and anywhere in the woodland or rock garden. With the exception of *Cyclamen europaeum*, they are not evergreen all through the year, but we are placing them here because some of their leaves are in their full beauty from the early autumn until the spring.

The large, ivy-shaped leaves of *C. neapolitanum* lie almost flat upon the ground, fascinating in their beauty, and from deep green to exquisitely marbled tones and silvery patterns. They stand up to all the shattering effects of winter's worst efforts. *Neapolitanum* blooms in the late summer and autumn, its flowers varying from pure white, and soft pink to rosy shades. In *C. orbiculatum coum* the leaves are rounded and dark green and appear in the autumn. Its gay little flowers, so unbelievably cheerful in deep magenta-red, brave the worst days of the New Year and continue well on into the spring. The flowers are shorter and tubbier than most cyclamen. It is followed by *C. repandum* in March, April and on to May; usually the dark green leaves appear before the scented flowers, which are a vivid carmine. Then comes the summer flowering evergreen *europaeum*, which is one of the best, its rosy-pink flowers being deliciously scented. It often starts blooming about June and where there is a group of them, it is not unusual to have some flowering on into December.

There are other cyclamen of varying degrees of hardiness, but mostly for warmer soils than ours, and these are also more for the connoisseur. Sometimes they are offered as dry corms which can be re-established, but they are often slow to do so; it is better to choose the smaller ones, they have a better chance when used for this purpose. We would always advocate pot grown ones!

Now just one more evergreen: *Rohdea japonica* which is good to look upon on any winter's day. It forms a low clump of 6-inch long, thick, leathery leaves which arch over like those of *Reineckia carnea*. This is an exciting newcomer to us, but its appearance alone is satisfying enough for it to be grown as a foliage plant. It is of the lily family and comes from Japan; it is said to bear short spikes of little white bells which may be followed by red berries. It is quite hardy, easily grown in a shady place, but is rare and may be difficult to come by.

✳ 5 ✳
Other Plants for Shade and Part Shade

In *Making a Shrub Garden*, we described some of the planting of our shrubs, but now as time has passed away and these are growing up to give us more shade and shelter to transform it gradually to semi-woodland, we are able to grow more plants that have a preference for these situations. Our paths also wind about the garden in all manner of ways, disappearing round bends rather like a flowing stream. With an odd birch, shrub or conifer at the stream bank as it were, this gives endless chances for unexpected surprises and many aspects for planting—shady, half-shady, and places where the late day sun is sufficient for certain plants. We find this semi-woodland gardening the most satisfying of all, for the range of plants varies from the ordinary to those which always arouse interest for their usefulness or rarity.

Woodland gardening may not be to all tastes, for it is an attempt at blending suitable plants into a natural setting, more than an aim to produce gaiety and masses of colour. Nevertheless, the meconopsis, primulas, astilbes, irises, mimulus and many others light up their territory in joyous abandon, especially if in generous groups. This chapter is mostly concerned with the plants which die down for the winter time, none the less these are often the most beautiful and those which give us a special thrill on reappearing in the joyful and lengthening days of spring.

Early upon the scene are the pulmonarias (lungworts), some beginning in March, and others dallying till early May. There is ample scope for some interesting collecting among these, in finding blue, red and white forms, the old 'soldiers and sailors', blue and pink flowered and many intermediate colours. Their great variety of handsome foliage, from *Pulmonaria angustifolia* with smooth leaves, to rough-leaved ones and others with lush spotted or marbled foliage, makes worth while and fascinating searching. Though they mostly die away in the winter, a collected form from the Alps which we were fortunate enough to be given, retains its dark green foliage beauty all the year. These are of the easiest cultivation in any reasonably moist soil, and fill in about woodland and shrub verges and all sorts of places where low growers are needed to cover the ground. *P. rubra* sets the ball rolling with large flowers of cheerful brick red, often blooming as early as late February. It is followed in March by *P. angustifolia*, with heads of bright blue; 'Munstead Blue' and 'Mawson's Variety' are other good blues. *P. a. alba*, a good snowy-white, comes along in the early days of May, but even then the others are still performing, so that red, white and blue may all be had together. *P. saccharata*, with pinky flowers, is more important for its startling foliage effect, for it has large, bold, light green leaves which are wonderfully marbled with white. It is generally evergreen, and is worth a prominent position and, undercarpeting fairly tall fuchsias such as 'Mrs Popple' with its dangling red flowers, the effect can be superb.

The bastard balm, which also might well be grown in the proximity of the pulmonarias for its later flowering, is an attractive plant which suffers as well under the name of *Melittis melissophyllum*. It has a pleasing old-world charm and was long cultivated for its healing properties, when its oil was applied to wounds. Again, this is a rare native of south-west England and South Wales, but is mainly found in the woodlands of southern Europe. It befits odd, part-shady corners or the shaded end of the border, where its unique charm would not compete with too colourful an array. Its white flowers are decorated with reddish-purple at the lip of a mimulus-like flower, a charming combination against its rough nettle-like leaves. A non-invasive and erect habit of a foot or so, together with its ability to be self-supporting, add to its virtues. Altogether, it is an intriguing plant; it appears above ground again in mid-March.

An unusual herbaceous perennial which grows alongside the latter is *Lysimachia ciliata* (syn. *Steironema ciliatum*) which we value not only for its very long flowering time, but as a memory to an old friend who had an eagle eye for the exceptional plant. Usually the loosestrife family err on the rampageous side, but *ciliata* is more refined in habit and flower. In early April when we begin to count our blessings for those plants returning once again to the earth's surface, this is just showing dark leaves at soil level. It is a shallow rooting plant which needs moist soil, and then it will creep quite slowly into a fairly compact clump. The first of its soft old gold flowers appear in early July and continue into the autumn when its flowering stems will have reached up to nearly 2 feet.

Another erect grower which is shallow rooting is *Mimulus ringens*; this looks well in company with the foregoing and comes into flower at the same time with large, gaping violet flowers. Another unusual monkey flower is *M. cardinalis*, which grows about 2 feet high and parades narrow scarlet blossoms from July to September. Sometimes self-sown seedlings will flower in the first year.

Our first introduction to the astrantias was in our old cottage garden where it was among the plants that survived years of neglect. It was *Astrantia major* which, like the rest stands erect and looks after itself, quite enough to recommend any plant! The flowers, which are an attractive greeny-pink, last a long time, and grow in clusters—each individual flower has a centre of many stamens surrounded by a papery frill, exactly like a miniature Victorian bouquet. It is a good foil to bright colours in a border and prefers a situation that is moist. In shade and among shrubs it shows up well on its own, and there its glossy leaves do not flag at the first effects of drought. There are others of these old-fashioned masterworts, much alike in flower but differing in stature and in their curiously fascinating shades of rosy-pinks and even reddish tones.

Though the calthas are waterside plants, we find that the double form, *Caltha palustris plena* does well at moist edges of the damper woodland, and if the weather be exceptionally dry, good soakings after flowering induce it to produce new growth. Its brilliant orange-yellow flowers make a glorious display in early April. Alongside this grows a member of the *Saxifragaceae* from

North America, *Boykinia aconitifolia* which looks very much in its right place, carpeting the woodland with its lush leaves. In April it sends up 2-foot stems on which are borne a host of creamy-white saxifrage-like flowers which are still in evidence in June.

For situations less moist than the calthas enjoy, we can recommend *Anemonopsis macrophylla*, not perhaps an 'everyday plant' and sometimes difficult to come by, but one for those with a taste for the unusual. It is just the plant to grow to the fore of shrubby bays which form a pseudo-woodland, where it will get the degrees of shade and uniform moisture that it will thrive on. It is a Japanese introduction, and has firm glossy leaves and handsome columbine-like flowers of unusually solid and waxy texture in a pale shade of lavender-blue in July. The blooms arch over gracefully from slender, but very springy 18-inch stems. In good deep, lime-free soil rich in humus, it is a good perennial, forming sturdy and satisfying clumps. It can be raised from seed, but it does not germinate until the second year.

The same situation suits the scopolias which are also among the uncommon and rare. Their role is with the large-leaved and distinctive, and it may be fulfilled often in problem places—sometimes difficult, dry-shade places, as long as the soil is not too poor. Borders on the shady side of the house are a very suitable situation, as their bell-shaped flowers are borne in spring, when perhaps one does not want to journey too far to see them. Rising to some 10–12 inches, *Scopolia carniolica* bears big bells of pale primrose-yellow and these swing gracefully from among the leaves. *S. podolica* is with us too, giving intriguing greenish-purple bells. Scopolias have the weird fascination of the hellebores in their strange shades, so much so, that the few others that there are, are well worth seeking if you find them appealing.

The Japanese toad lilies—*Tricyrtis*—also come under the category of the curiously quaint, and with the exceptions of *Tricyrtis macropoda* and *T. latifolia*, they add their contribution to the welcome flowers of the late autumn. Though they can be recommended to those who like to acquire lesser-known plants, their particular beauty might not be appreciated by all, for though their flowers are lily-like and waxen in texture, they are spotted and freckled and some are arrayed in sombre colours of purple and mauve. *T. hirta* is perhaps the best known, with large, handsome, creamy-white flowers flecked with purple. Blooming in late September, it will grow up to 18 inches. In the shady border, the strong growing *T. macropoda* is admirable for its bold foliage and the way its expanded flowers are held erect on 1½-2-foot stems. The flowers which come along in June are large and greenish-yellow with purple mottling. There is much to be said for these, for they keep to themselves, do not ramp about and are easily grown.

Solomon's seal (*Polygonatum multiflorum*) is one of the striking architectural plants which always looks right in a woodland setting or the part-shady walks. It has the great merit of growing and filling in shady places among trees where often other plants will not flower. Its great charm is in its elegant 2–3-foot arching stems with shiny leafage of glaucous-green and the rows of flowers that dangle and hang so gracefully. Usually in twos and threes, these cylindrically shaped flowers are creamy-white, green tipped with all nature's artistry, and are suspended from the leaf axils of each leaf in May. It is the most decorative of the family, especially in blossom, but for the collector of singular plants there is the enchanting double form of *P. officinale*. This is a smaller, dainty, slow-growing plant for a choice place in half-shade. The pointed-leaved *P. verticillatum*, though not very conspicuous in flower, is especially worth growing as a handsome foliage attraction.

Some near relations to these Solomon's seals are the smilacinas, woodland plants of Europe and North America. These also have a creeping rhizomatous rootstock and much the same graceful habit. Our first essay with these was *Smilacina stellata* which produces small clusters of white flowers on foot-high stems in late spring. It is an ideal carpeter for running about among rhododendrons and in thin woodland. From time to time we have tried to obtain *S. racemosa*, which is by far the most impressive of them. Finally, we managed to get seed of it and after taking a year to germinate, it flowered for the first time at three years old. Though a much stronger growing plant than *stellata*, its great merit is in its compactness and a showy creamy plume of flowers which are delightfully scented. Its stem rises to 2½ feet, arching gracefully over and bearing bright red berries in the autumn. It is easily grown and is an especially choice plant for moist shade.

One of our successes and great favourites in the garden is *Orchis maderensis* (syn. *O. foliosa*), indeed one of the noblest of this exalted family. Every year it gives us and others such joy with more and more of its sturdy 2-foot spikes of bloom, putting up magnificent, concentrated heads of rich wine-purple 9–10 inches long, a display that lasts for many weeks from mid-June. Would that more of these were so easy to grow for, unlike other hardy terrestrial orchids, provided that its position is slightly shaded and reasonably moist, it does not fuss about getting just the right mycorrhiza to live upon. No doubt our rotted bracken compost plays its part in keeping an open friable mixture for plants like this, but nevertheless, in seven to eight years from one crown, it has spread widely as well as yielding a few for friends. It is imperturbably hardy, and even by early December, shoots are showing at ground level yearning for better days when they can forge ahead. We are fortunate also to have the familiar early purple spotted *O. maculata* upon our ground in its varying forms and the delightful summer flowering, sweetly scented ladies' tresses (*Spiranthes spiralis*).

In these shady places and woodland glades there is no more lovely sight than a drift of the ever popular blue poppy, *Meconopsis betonicifolia* (syn. *M. baileyi*)—thanks be to courageous plant collectors. One never fails to marvel every year that this Himalayan beauty should look so happy so far away from its mountain homeland. If certain principles are followed, it is a very good perennial, forming hearty clumps that carry on for a number of years. Like most of these meconopsis it likes rich well-drained soil that does not dry out—in general the same conditions that many of the primulas enjoy. In light soils the ground should be well prepared with the addition of leaf-soil and even some handfuls of crumbled manure below, as they are deep rooting. In heavier soils it is important that the surface of the soil around them is porous so that excessive winter wet does not rot the crowns. Half an inch of grit or very sharp sand around them will ensure this and also allow for a topdressing of bonemeal or powdered manure to be easily washed in by rain. Young plants will often bloom the first year, this does no harm as long as the heads are cut off immediately after flowering so that it does not exhaust itself in forming seed. Better still if you can be ruthless, stop them flowering, your fortitude will be rewarded by stronger plants that will form good crowns to each plant and a longer life in all.

Meconopsis betonicifolia grows up to 3–4 feet with branching stems and many 3–4-inch-wide flowers of a ravishing kingfisher blue with a central boss of yellow stamens. A wind sheltered position is ideal, as often there are blustery winds in late May when they are in flower.

Meconopsis quintuplinervia, Farrer's harebell poppy, is a sound perennial with a running, clump forming habit. It does not require full shade, but rather, coolness at the root. Without the height and magnificence of *betonicifolia* it is more easily placed among the smaller rhododendrons and dwarf shrubs which give its roots sufficient ground shade. What it may lack in grandeur compared with *betonicifolia*, it more than makes up in loveliness and the elegant poise of its bell-shaped flowers. Its slender stems rise 15–18 inches, bearing globular, nodding lavender-blue, poppy-like blossoms. It may safely be divided in the spring, or after flowering, in which case it should be kept moist for a week or so.

Another perennial poppy, which is rarely seen and certainly ought to be grown more, is *M. villosa* which was at one time under cultivation by the name of *Cathcartia villosa* long before the blue poppy ever became popular. While *quintuplinervia* is deciduous, the inclusion of *villosa* in the same bed can give a winter furnishing of rosettes of golden-brown hairy leaves that are more encouraging to look upon in the dormant months. It forms a handsome looking clump that changes in late spring, when new pale green, much-lobed leaves are rising to shelter the flowering stems. At flowering time these are 18 inches and the nodding golden-yellow flowers, much like the Welsh poppy, continue for many weeks after the blue poppy has finished. It seeds freely and germinates well, the resulting plants flowering in their second year.

The pale yellow Welsh poppy, *M. cambrica*, our only native meconopsis—a perennial—needs little describing; we love it here and there to fill up shady places. Some admire the orange form, it is a matter of personal taste, but the colour does not seem to harmonize in a woodland setting. There is also a double yellow and a double orange for the searching, but we do not find them half so attractive. We have no great experience of the other beauties of the family, beyond a few of the monocarpic kind such as *napaulensis* and *integrifolia* which flowered and seeded upon us when we were garden making and had less time to replace them by resowing.

A near relation of these meconopsis is *Stylophorum diphyllum*, the celandine poppy, an aristocrat among these for part shade or cool places. Beyond this it has no peculiar requirements and is amenable in every way, even to being carefully divided in spring time. It is very distinguished, having soft blue-grey hairy leaves, and its 4-petalled flowers hang gracefully in clusters from 12–15-inch stems. In May and June the clear golden-yellow, poppy-like, cup-shaped blossoms are borne in moderate profusion. It is clump forming and can be equally at home in the shady part of any border. Though dying away in the autumn, by the New Year, a nice fat nobbly crown will assure you that there are good things to come.

Handsome foliage plants are deservedly more appreciated now, and one of the most striking examples are the veratrums with their bold, clear green corrugated leaves which fan outwards in great opulent ovals. They are very satisfying as spectacular plants and demand isolation to create the best picture. They do not appear above ground until March, and by late May the extra-ordinary beauty of their leaves is fully unfolded. From these arise towering spires of 4–5 feet with branching panicles massed with starry flowers. They flower from late July into August; in the case of *Veratrum nigrum* they are purplish-maroon, and greenish-yellow in *V. album*. In spite of their height, the stems are so sturdy and well anchored that we have never had to stake them. They look right in part shade thrusting up and above dwarf shrubs, but if the soil be deep and moist, which they enjoy, some sun is not resented. Carpets of the dwarf *Tiarella cordifolia* or *Ajuga reptans* 'Atropurpurea' in the foreground can create a pleasing picture.

In the same class of outstanding foliage plants are the hostas, the plantain lilies, or funkias as they were once known. One's taste in plants can change with the years, for whereas at one time we did not appreciate them and almost despised them, possibly associating them with the Victorian era of gardening, now we both appreciate the aesthetic value of their foliage. Their virtues are more apparent, in particular the great difference in leaf-form and colouring, and furthermore, in a garden too large in some ways, they do a job for us in covering the ground, completely smothering any weeds or weed seedlings and helping to destroy our enemy the sorrel. Apart from their handsome leaves, they produce funnel-shaped flowers in the summer and the early autumn, and add a very good turn of colour in their dying foliage. They are very hardy, long-lived and, once planted, require no cultural aid. Some shade and a good moist soil are their main requirements, though they will often flower with great freedom in sunshine as long as the soil does not dry out, but when growing by the water or pond side they are supremely happy.

Two robust growers with bold foliage are *Hosta sieboldiana*, having glaucous, grey-green, deeply veined leaves with bells of pale mauve, and *H. fortunei* with pale green leaves and pale lilac bells on 2-foot stems rising well above the foliage. The cultivar *H. fortunei albopicta* spears the ground in April with startling bright yellow, green-edged leaves, gradually unfolding its beauty to a paler yellow, which by mid-summer fades to a pale yellowish-green. *H.* 'Aurea Maculata' (now *H. fortunei aurea*) also greets the early months with pale yellow, long-pointed leaves which gradually turn to green in the later summer when lavender flowers are borne on foot-high stems.

Hosta ventricosa is distinct in forming a compact dark-leaved clump, sending up very erect 2–2½-foot stems with many large, open lily-like bells of mauve lasting well into the early autumn. *H. lancifolia* is medium sized, with dark green, sharply pointed leaves. Slender stems hold up violet-mauve bells which hang gracefully downwards over its mass of prostrate leaves; it is also later flowering. *H. l. albomarginata* with larger leaves than the latter, is a decorative plant with green and white margined leaves. This flowers at the end of June and has short spikes of soft mauve flowers. Another unusual white variegated plant is *H. undulata* with wavy, curled leaves, green edged and having internal bands of clear white. It is a small, low-growing plant with lilac flowers on 10–12-inch stems. We find it is best in shade or part shade as

94

too much sun is apt to brown the edges of the leaves and spoil its unusual form.

One that we consider the most attractive is *H. crispula* with good upstanding, veined leaves of sage green. A pure white border to the slightly waved leaves gives it an air of distinction, and in July it produces broadly funnel-shaped flowers. A plant we have as *H. decora* 'Thomas Hogg' is also very fine, a little larger in the foliage than the latter, but also with broad white margins to the leaves; flowering at the same time, it is distinguished by its dark lilac trumpets.

Most beautiful is the autumn-flowering *H. plantaginea*, with sumptuous, pure white, solid textured, wide open bells which yield a delicious scent. Our own forms a clump of almost prostrate long-pointed leaves, a pleasant enough carpet of greenery throughout the summer, but a friend has a further cultivar with exceptionally large heart-shaped leaves—we wait patiently for a small division that has been booked! At first ours was in part shade and we were disappointed at its lack of flower, but learning that it should be in full sun, we moved it and in its first year of full sunshine we were rewarded by an immediate and thrilling response. Flowering as late as September, it needs warmth and moisture to accelerate its flowering.

Two small species for choice places where treasures can be watched, are *H. tardiflora* and *H. albomarginata alba*. Tardiflora is a dainty late flowering kind with quite small dark green leaves and slender 6–8-inch spikes of lilac flowers. *H. albomarginata alba* is new to us, but is obviously dwarf, and had white flowers on 10–12-inch stems in September. Slugs are rather partial to hostas, so that it is a good policy to make a war upon them before the leaves have grown very much in the spring.

The day lilies (*Hemerocallis*), so very close to the hostas in the family tree, are mentioned under Favourite Herbaceous Perennials in Chapter 2, but they are so easy going that a reminder is made here of their assets for shade or part shade.

That we still have our original plant of *Saxifraga fortunei*, bought before the Second War, says much for its sound constitution. Now it is a goodly sized clump, a large lowly mass of broad, glossy, rounded foliage. In our undulating garden we are able to grow it in a raised shady pocket where a waft of wind may occasionally lift its leaves enough to reveal wonderful maroon undersides. It does not flower till early October, when its flowering stems arise erect to 10–12 inches. Each individual flower is by no means shapely, but the branching stems bear such a mass of pure white stars that the whole gives quite a scintillating effect. Unfortunately, an autumn frost can reduce it to pulp; on the other hand we have seen it flower many more times than it has been spoilt. In spite of any setback, late April will see it cheerfully back to full leaf again. It comes from Japan, as also the allied *S. cortusifolia*, another species of this rather neglected group of Diptera saxifrages. They have their own charm and distinction and earn a chosen place. *Cortusifolia* has fine glossy, dark green, rounded leaves and starry white flowers some four weeks earlier than *fortunei*; the form *cortusifolia* 'Rosea' may quench the thirst of those who need a little more colour. It is the daintiness of these various saxifrage species that led us to a fancy for them; they look so right in shady pockets, light woodland or even a shady mixed border of special plants. The compact growing *S. rotundifolia* is one such, and after its winter rest it sends up fleshy rounded leaves and slender branching stems of 18 inches with a myriad of white flowers flecked with pink. An evergreen one is *S. geum*, one of the London Pride persuasion with showers of pink flowers. More of a carpeter for the fringes, it does this with a hearty mat of long-stalked, spoon-shaped leaves which assume yellow and orange tones in the autumn. A neat tuft-forming, very miniature London pride is *cuneifolia*, a huddle of dark evergreen leaves which erupt miniature sprays of pure white blossoms. Yet another to revel in a shady sanctum is *S. hypnoides*' the Dovedale moss, which is lit up in May with a profusion of white flowers. It is of the freshest green that we so appreciate in winter time.

One acquires a taste for these lesser plants for intimate places and quiet woodland niches where some shade helps to give them the coolness which they thrive upon. Another peep into the saxifrage family gives us the sweet *Heuchera racemosa*. It is an attractive little species from America, and forms neat evergreen clumps of graceful leaves; in June it sends up 6-inch stems which bear thick racemes of charming, creamy-white flowers. The leaves of *H.*

micrantha are much smaller, dark green and sit close to the ground in a tight little clump. It is a dainty, fairy plant of especial charm if one can admire and appreciate the Lilliputian. It bears airy, 10–12-inch panicles of small white flowers.

Of the same family is the diminutive *Mitella breweri*, which grows into the tidiest of prostrate spreading mats of dark rounded leaves, so close that they all seem joined together. Winter never seems to marr the shiny greenness of its carpet, and in summer its short racemes dangle little fringed cups of greenish-white flowers. There are a number more of these pocket-sized heucheras and mitellas which take up little room, so that if you have a fancy for lowly treasures, they are worth seeking.

Kirengeshoma palmata is in a much larger class, a senior representative of the saxifrage family, and though by no means an 'every-day plant', can usually be found in one of a dozen or so catalogues, or often inquiries at the various horticultural shows will unearth these less common plants. Also a Japanese plant, it will flourish in any shady place as long as it is in good moist soil. It is unique in every way, perhaps the most architectural and spectacular plant of the shade lovers, its dark stems arching gracefully over when in full growth and bearing sprays of cool yellow, bell-shaped flowers backed by soft green, vine-like foliage which finally yellows to the cool of autumn days. It may be slow to establish, but when settled down forms a dense, slowly widening clump from which its stems arise to 2 feet at flowering time in September, after which it dies away completely.

When a wood has been cleared, what more lovely sight than the mass of our own native foxgloves (*Digitalis purpurea*) that so often spring up and present such a rosy picture to the evening sunshine. For a mere pinch of scattered seed, no less a picture can soon be had in the garden. As long as these are kept in the background, too much weeding out of unwanted seedlings can be avoided. There are the 'Excelsior' and 'Shirley' strains to choose from, but for us it is the wild species, and also those lovely pure white and pale pink varieties which crop up from time to time, that are the real charmers. Yet there are others that bring delight, and a good outstanding and perennial one that has come to the fore is *D. mertonensis*, 3 feet high and with flowers of a crushed strawberry

G

shade in June. Another perennial species of 1½–2 feet is *D. ambigua*, with fat bells of soft brownish-yellow in summer time; this sows itself about in a mild way. The 'seed-sowers' may well try others, mostly biennials, but all very interesting and easy. *D. ferruginea* is tall with a basal rosette of very narrow leaves and unusual flowers of brownish-red borne on a long tapering spike.

From the mountains of Korea, which has produced so many first-class hardy plants, we have *Aceriphyllum rossii*. It is not for the rough and tumble of border oddments, but rather for the favourite place with plants of unique interest. It does not appear above ground till late March and then gradually unfolds a low rosette of large shiny, maple-like leaves. Above these, foot-high pink flower stems hold a flat panicle with masses of white, saxifrage-like flowers. Alongside we grow another pretty and permanent woodlander, *Dentaria polyphylla* from our near Eastern Alps. It is yet another neat clump forming plant which is quite hardy and easy and a good subject to grow at the shady side of the house. Happy in the same cool soil as its near relatives, the cardamines, it is also one of the chief delights of April days. Once well established it sends up a thicket of strong 15-inch stems with handsome foliage and carrying at the top, heads of snowy-white flowers; it goes to rest fairly soon after flowering.

Once one has succumbed to the fascination of these smaller woodland plants, one finds at the end of the catalogues, a member of the exalted *Liliacae*, the charming *Uvularia grandiflora* from American woodlands. Considering its ease of cultivation and some likeness to the admirable erythroniums, it is surprising that it is not more often seen, for it comes along with the very welcome late spring flowers and associates well with other shade lovers such as anemones, primroses and the erythroniums. It shows above ground in early May and then in a matter of a few weeks, quite large, clear yellow, pendant bells hang in clusters from 9–12-inch stems. In a cool spot and leafy soil, it forms hearty, everlasting clumps. America is rich in these woodland perennials and among those taking kindly to our climate are the actaeas. Though not commonly grown, their spikes of white flowers show up well in the shady places that they like. While they are fairly vigorous growing and leafy, compactness is one of their virtues. Failing a shady spot in the woodland, the moist side of the house often asks for such a fill-up plant. *Actaea spicata*, also native of the north of England, puts up spikes of almost a yard, and the flowers are succeeded by very handsome red or white berries, but a fair warning must be given, for they are poisonous.

Few gardens are without our own lovely native primrose (*Primula vulgaris*), and *P.* 'Wanda', and its great variety of children which give real colour so early in the year and do such a good job of clump-forming for edgings and for the rock garden. The old *P. denticulata* also runs them very close in popularity as well as the trusty *P. japonica* which must have been in cultivation almost a hundred years. The latter belongs to the Candelabra group of these primulas, most of which rise to some 2–3 feet with whorls of flowers at regular intervals up the stems. These are the ones which look well in drifts in the shade of shrubs and by the waterside and places that occur in the shadow of houses and neighbouring trees in town gardens. The majority of these primulas are easily raised from seed and most rewarding in generally flowering within a year from sowing.

Besides *P. japonica*, others in the Candelabra group are just as accommodating, provided they have part shade during the day and a good, deep, moist soil which will benefit from a little manure dug into it. *P. helodoxa* we have already mentioned with the evergreen woodlanders. It likes plenty of moisture, naturalizes itself well and individual plants are long lived.

The rich crimson *P. pulverulenta* is another robust species, arresting with its large leaves and mealy white stems rising to 3 feet. *P. pulverulenta* 'Red Hugh' is a selected colour form which flourishes equally well and breeds reasonably true from seed. At one time we grew *P. beesiana*, a 2 foot high species with tiers of vivid magenta flowers, but this has interbred so much that it is difficult to obtain true now. One of the earliest too, was *P. bulleyana* with large, very serrated leaves and strong stems bearing whorls of orange-yellow flowers in June.

The Sikkimensis group are among our favourites for their delicate scent and elegant drooping flowers which earns them the name of giant cowslips. Apart from their nodding bells they are variable in colour range and height. *P. sikkimensis* itself, with clustered heads of pale yellow bells, closely resembles our native cowslip, except that these are gracefully held on 2-foot high stems. Its neat tuft of leaves usually spears the ground by April when *Meconopsis betonicifolia* is already well in leaf, but ere May is out, both are flowering together. It is an easily grown primula, sowing itself and flowering quickly. The lovely *P. secundiflora* is even more striking in its modestly drooping wine-crimson to burgundy coloured bells, and its 10–12-inch stems are beautifully painted with white meal. Although this is a good plant to grow alongside *sikkimensis* as it flowers a little later, we cherish it so much that it gets the best of well drained places.

The giant of the section is *P. florindae*, some say it grows up to 4 feet if it gets all the moisture that it requires, and then it can be very lush in foliage. It is a popular waterside primula, and a group with their tall stems bearing a large head of almost countless yellow cowslip flowers, is most satisfying, especially as its flowering period is from July to August. It is a reliable perennial which will thrive well in shade. No doubt its hybrids in reddish and apricot shades have their admirers, but to us they miss the appeal of the type plant. In the same group *P. alpicola* steps down to a mere 12–15 inches, a charmer with nodding fragrant flowers of pale creamy-white which earn it the romantic title of the moonlight primula. Then there is its coloured form, *P. alpicola* 'Violacea' with violet-purple flowers. These die away in the autumn, but return again by mid-April, all ready to flower in June. Though these are natives of boggy places in Tibet, they are precious plants which are safeguarded by sharply drained moist places. Both of these and the delectable *secundiflora* are good subjects for shady pockets of the rock garden.

Other primulas of merit which may also be mentioned as suitable for the moist shady parts of the rock garden are *P. involucrata* and its close and charming relation *P. rosea*. The happy, colourful *rosea* is the delight of earliest spring, when its gay rosy-pink flowers will brighten the days of March and April. It grows just as well in sun or shade, provided there is plenty of moisture at the root, and will soon make hearty clumps. *P. involucrata*, like *rosea*, will endure fairly wet conditions. Its 10–12-inch flower stems bear an umbel of deliciously scented creamy-white flowers in early summer.

Primula sieboldii from Japan, and almost one of the longest in cultivation in this country, was at one time used as a greenhouse plant. As a result of this some doubts may have arisen as to its hardiness, but we have found it very durable, and easily grown, but all the better for an occasional division. Its low tufts of soft, heart-shaped leaves are quite beautiful and the flowers are borne in loose heads, usually about 6 inches high. It is variable from rose and rosy-purple to pink and white.

To add to these we must mention the primulas known as 'Inshriach hybrids' which are always so much admired. This is a hearty race with a wonderful range of colours in orange, pinks, yellows and terra-cotta shades. A group make a lovely picture and are quite irresistible, with their distinct yet soft colourings that blend nicely together. Just one more is the beautiful *P. chionantha* of the Nivales section, the plants of which are generally regarded as rather difficult, more so in the south of England. *Chionantha* is the easiest of them and we find it amenable as long as it has a cool shady pocket where it is well drained; some of ours have lasted for years. It is a plant of quality and loveliness in flower, with the creamy-white, scented flowers dangling from 18-inch stems, and the whole plant is powdered with white meal. The species we have mentioned are but a few of the many hundred that can be grown, but they are all first-rate garden plants—so many of the others need extra care and frequent re-raising from seed.

Very often it happens that the attractive and lovely plants that we should like to grow prove to be difficult, half-hardy or intractable in some way. Not so the roscoeas, with their fascinating likeness to the beautiful flowers of orchids—their similarity has earned them the title of 'poor man's orchid', for their reasonable price and easy ways. They are lovers of shady or part shady positions such as pockets between small or medium-sized shrubs, and look well among rhododendrons or on the shadier side of the rock garden. The soil should be rich, moist and well drained and, given that, they will even stand quite a bit of sunshine. They are tuberous rooted plants that come from China. The species which are generally available from nurseries are *Roscoea alpina*, *R.*

cautleoides, R. *humeana*, R. *purpurea* and the newer variety R. *p. procera*, and are usually supplied as pot grown, but if received as tubers they should be planted 5–6 inches deep. All have a special attraction in their interesting fresh green foliage which is very leek-like in appearance, and their particular charm lies in the two-lipped, curiously shaped flowers. They are tardy risers and it is late May, or even June if it is a cold season, before some of them appear above ground, but they develop rapidly and are often in flower within a few weeks.

Roscoea cautleoides is the one usually seen, for it is easily obtained and being a good grower, increases well, often seeding itself. It is singularly lovely for the delicate softness of its clear yellow flowers. The blossoms come in late May or early June and they stand up strongly from the 12–15-inch stem or sheath of fresh green which bears up to three flowers opening in succession. R. *humeana* is the largest-flowered, a most striking and exotic flower. In *The Present Day Rock Garden*, Clay speaks of this having: 'less grace than cautleoides, but with a more imperial splendour', and indeed it is most showy. This robust species produces its flowers in June and July from a strong, leek-like stem from which the large lush leaves develop, sometimes up to a foot or more in height. The flowers are a rich wine-purple, with the usual long lip and upper petals standing erect, the distinctive structure which makes them so curiously fascinating. R. *purpurea* is also fairly large in flower, a good grower and gay with its magenta-purple flowers, perhaps less attractive than the latter, or maybe surpassed by its grandeur. In its variety *procera*, however, we have a newer plant of exceptional allurement with flowers of a softer shade, and some forms are white with purple markings. R. *alpina* is a much smaller plant, the dwarf of the family, and very variable in form, generally met with as pink-flowered, though there are forms with purple or lavender blossoms. All these flowers are much smaller than the preceding, though large for the size of the plant, and seem to hover over the leaves like small butterflies. Although only single flowered, they are borne in a long succession from June to the end of July, held on 6-inch stems. With the leaves a little deeper green than *cautleoides alpina* is equally accommodating, appearing every year without attention. All of these may be increased by careful division when the clumps become too thick, the best time being in the spring just before they are in active growth.

Under the same conditions the podophyllums will thrive and can be recommended for handsomeness of leaf and ornamental fruits. They are unusual one-time members of the berberis family (now in their own family *Podophyllaceae*), not for 'window-dressing', but chiefly for those who appreciate the beauty of foliage. In this, *Podophyllum emodii* from the Himalayas is the most attractive with large, handsomely marbled leaves which gradually develop to as much as 6–8 inches across. These leaves are folded backwards like a closed umbrella as they push through in the early spring, but soon the flower bud appears and opens out to a cupped flower of lovely apple blossom pink. As the elegant pale green foliage gradually expands and the stem thrusts them up to 12 inches or so, the marking on the leaves becomes more pro-minent. Maybe it is forgotten, many other beautiful things take one's attention, time passes, then suddenly in the autumn its huge fruits are in evidence—as large as a small hen's egg! *P. peltatum* from America sends up pale green parasols, unspotted but up to 15–18 inches in height, and bears white flowers and small yel-lowish-green fruits. It has beauty if room can be found for it, but it cannot compete with *emodii*.

The berberis family gives us an unusual and precious wood-lander and spring flowerer in *Jeffersonia dubia* (syn. *Plagiorhegma dubia*) from Manchuria. It is a favourite of the spring show benches at Westminster and though it is perfectly hardy, for years we cherished it as an alpine house plant, but when war came it had to go into the open ground. But here its beauty can be enjoyed just as well in April days. Then its very lovely inch-wide, soft lavender-blue flowers come on 3-inch stems while the leaves are unfolding, these, too, are no small part of its attraction, for they are large, rounded and glaucous, so gently balanced on wiry stems. If grown in a very cool position there is less likelihood of the leaves rising to obscure the flowers. It retires below ground in the autumn and is best planted in the peat bed or where other choice plants are grown.

The erythroniums often take their place in moistish rock

garden pockets even though their natural place is in part-shady woodland. They are ideal spring flowering dwarf plants for the margins of part-shady woodland or border where they are of easy cultivation, long-lived and when well suited will regenerate themselves. Their graceful, reflexed flowers which pass through a very colourful range, suggest some beautiful miniature lily.

The most easily obtainable, and the species which is generally grown is *Erythronium dens-canis*, so called because of the likeness of the tubers to a dog's tooth. Apart from this one which occurs in other parts of the world, the remainder are native to the eastern, western and North American States, all of them belonging to the lily family. *E. dens-canis* varies in colour from white to carmine and rosy-purples, and the leaves of most of them are beautifully mottled. They increase rapidly, though we do not find them so free flowering as the American species. Of the latter, *E. californicum*, one of the most beautiful, gives us a drift of pale yellow, the flowers being almost 2 inches across. It is very free flowering and holds as many as 6–7 flowers to a stem and has finely mottled leaves. For sheer beauty *E. revolutum* 'White Beauty' is a real joy, with creamy-white reflexed flowers on 10–12-inch stems. Another fine cultivar is *E. revolutum* 'Johnsoni' with large rose-pink flowers and finely marked foliage.

Among those with bright yellow blossoms and plain green foliage are *E. tuolumnense* and *E. grandiflorum*. The former increases well but does not flower so freely unless confined in a rock garden pocket or in poorer soil. *E. hendersonii* will always be one of our favourites for its lovely flowers of pale rose with a purple centre. It is taller than most, rising up to 15 inches and bearing as many as 5–6 flowers to a stem; it also multiplies well. These are but a few of the treasures that may be laid at your feet; unfortunately too few are offered, so it is as well to snap up any without hesitation if you are proffered a basket full. Sometimes specialist seedsmen list some of the species and this can be rewarding to the adventurous gardener who will see them flower in two to three years.

The hardy white arum of the hedgerows is always a worthy ornament for the garden and is happy enough tucked away at the base of shrubs, giving a fine show of orange-red fruits after it has flowered. But an exciting one to search for is *Arum creticum* from

Crete, also completely hardy. This has large, spear-shaped leaves which peep up early in the year, and by March the flowers are thrust upwards to show an exceedingly handsome spathe and spadix of lemon-yellow, a really grand sight when it is well established and thrusting up numbers of them. It likes a cool, well-drained position and is a showy plant to have on the cool side of the house. The other well-known arum, the popular greenhouse plant with its pure white 'arums' and large leaves, alas, can only be trusted outside in the warmest gardens. Fortunately there is a hardy form of this named *Zantedeschia* 'Crowborough', identical in beauty of leaf and flower. Standing up to almost 3 feet, the pure white flowers put a touch of splendour to any lightly shaded corner or a sunny moist spot. Though this cultivar is hardy, young plants should be nursed through severe weather with a mulch of bracken.

However bold and magnificent some plants may be, we never cease to be delighted by the elfin beauty of some of the smaller irises, *I. verna*, *I. cristata* and *I. gracilipes*. *I. verna* is one of the pygmy species that will always be scarce, for it increases so slowly that it does not easily submit to being cut into pieces for propagation and we have never yet known it set seed. Possibly it does not even yield much seed in its native eastern United States, for neither have we seen any offered. Its exquisite little flowers of violet-blue are made strikingly attractive by a brilliant orange band on the falls. At only 3 inches it is in balanced proportion to the 3–4-inch-long, green shiny leaves which lie almost prostrate upon the ground. We view this with great anticipation when about the middle of April it shows signs of buds. It is the only time that slugs may be troublesome and spoil the blooms, so that these sacrilegious orgies have to be anticipated by a little slug slaying. *I. verna* is a woodland plant in nature, but succeeds where it is moist in part shade away from the hottest sun.

On the other hand, our other favourite dwarf, *I. cristata* is much easier and seems to flower more freely with some sunshine. It is a bare 3 inches when blooming in May, with quite large lavender-blue flowers decorated with white and gold. When well suited, odd flowers will be produced through the summer. It spreads well and its close growing fans of pale green, low foliage are always a pleasure to look upon. *I. cristata* 'Alba' is exquisitely beautiful and as vigorous as the type.

The other beauty, *I. gracilipes* from Japan, is another natural woodlander which we have always counted among our successes by growing on the shady side of shrubs or sometimes more in the open where a nearby rock will conserve moisture for its roots. The flowers are pale and we think show up better in the shade, or is it that they light up the shade with their lavender and gold? None could fail to appreciate the beauty, elegance and breeding in the erect poise of its flowers and delicately arching light green leaves. These irises are shallow rooting and when new roots are sent out after flowering, it is of the greatest benefit to topdress them with a layer of fresh soil.

Plants which are trouble free and appear year after year without any need of cultural attention are really good garden friends. Among these trusty ones we class *Trillium grandiflorum*, for some 30 years have passed since our first investment in them and they are still with us, now a considerably increased family. Once in suitable quarters, with rich woodland soil—cool places between shrubs and even sunless places are good—it steadily multiplies and flowers every year. *T. grandiflorum* is handsome in its foliage which rises in early May and is soon followed by its large, snow-white, 3-petalled flowers which stand prominently above the broad leaves. The flowers are 3–4 inches across, gradually fading to pink as they age, after which the whole plant soon goes to rest for another year. There are other species to be tried, all of them American woodlanders of charm and distinction.

The dodecatheons are another reliable and long-lived family which are very happy in thin shade where there is good moist soil. These are known as American cowslips or shooting stars, and are related to the primrose. Considering how easily they are grown and the general popularity of spring flowers, it is surprising that they are not greater favourites. The flowers have a quaint beauty of their own, each petal of the blossoms being reflexed and grace-fully poised like those of the cyclamen. *Dodecatheon meadia* is the best known, strongly growing up to 18 inches, and with the naked scape bearing an umbel of some twenty or more flowers at the top, which vary from pink and rose to white. In form the flowers of the different species scarcely vary, and there is little distinction between them, with the exception of some of the dwarf species. *D. alpinum* is one of these, a pretty plant with 6–8-inch stems which carry clusters of pink flowers in May. *D. pauci-florum*, another worthy species, carries its rosy-mauve flowers on 10–12-inch stems, but there are fewer to the head than *D. meadia*. *D. latifolium* differs from the others in having a basal tuft of very broad rounded leaves, flat upon the ground, and the flowers are richly coloured rosy-pink. As with the trilliums, these all die away a few weeks after flowering.

Some of the most neglected of the lily family, and deserving to be in every garden, are the anthericums of the European alpine meadows, grassy-leaved plants which have elegant, white, trumpet-shaped blooms. In spite of their hardiness, ease of cultivation and exceptional merits, they have never yet become common plants. *Anthericum liliago*, known as the St. Bernard's lily, sends up foot-high stems with pure white, lily-like flowers. *A. liliastrum* (more correctly known as *Paradisea liliastrum*), known as the St. Bruno's lily is larger, and with a splendid exotic head of blossoms of pure white carried on 1½–2-foot stems. *A. ramosum*, though smaller flowered, is a charming plant and the 2-foot spike and side branches all bear inch-wide pure white, starry flowers. All these bloom in June and July and have a liking for a coolish position, part shade, or a moist border where they are useful to succeed earlier flowering plants.

The astilbes are ideal for massing in moist woodland, part shade or by the streamside. Though they are thirsty plants and grow luxuriously where there is plenty of moisture, they will generally do well in a border which does not become too dry in summer. Handsome and fine of foliage, and forming close clumps, they are ideal as ground-cover and to exclude weeds. They are the answer to a busy gardener's prayer, for so little is needed in the way of upkeep, and they can be very easily divided in the spring. For a floral effect of feathery flowers and close heads there is little to compare with them in the later summer. Whereas at one time their choice of colour was limited to whites and creams, now there is such a wonderful range of soft and bright colour in tall and shorter varieties that vistas through the woodland can compare with the azalea pageant in the spring. It would be superfluous to attempt to name and describe them, so many can be seen at shows or selected from nurserymen's catalogues.

The trollius or globe flowers are also moisture lovers but, provided the soil is moist, they appreciate some sunshine, or will grow in thin shade. They are trusty perennials that care for themselves, and their erect stems do not need staking. The flowers vary from yellow and creamy-yellow to orange and are mostly globular in shape. Our native, *Trollius europaeus*, is the best known and has lemon-yellow flowers in May, but there are now many cultivars between yellow and orange, and these extend the flowering time into June.

The finest of the species is *T. ledebouri* which is much later flowering and has very large, rich orange globes on 2–3-foot stems. *T. yunnanensis* is smaller and very useful among the front line plants where it is moist. It is only 10–12 inches tall but its charm is in its flat-open flowers of golden-yellow which are produced in June. *T. ranunculinus* (syn. *T. patulus*) also has wide open flowers on foot-high stems. The baby of the family is *T. pumilus* at 6 inches, a charming little species with flat-open flowers of golden-yellow. A moist pocket of the rock garden is the safest place for this pygmy.

✳ 6 ✳

Architectural Plants

BY JUDICIOUS PLACING, practically any plant can be accentuated by the grouping of plants around it and be made a picture on its own. Generally though, it is the bold, the showy or exotic looking plant that makes a beautiful or arresting incident. Though the imagination usually calls for floral effect, as we have said before, sheer colour can be blatant and needs relief, as can be given by foliage of distinct character. We need to appreciate colour in the foliage of plants, their form and build, their architectural shape for picturesque effect. There are plenty of plants to fill this role, even medium and small ones, but this is mostly a selection of taller plants.

One such example, *Dierama pulcherrima* we have already dealt with under Chapter 1, Some Sun-lovers and Exotics. It is indeed singularly picturesque as a specimen.

Acanthus mollis is perhaps a classic example of an architectural plant in more ways than one, for its leaf shape has been immortalized on the Greek Corinthian columns. It is worth growing for its foliage alone, and *A. mollis* 'Latifolius' is the most handsome form with very large, glossy green, leathery leaves which cover the ground. Its stalwart flower spikes will grow up to 4–5 feet, stiff and erect, bearing many purplish and white foxglove-like flowers from June onwards. It is a fine background plant, effective at the bend of a border or even as a single specimen on the lawn. In sun and good soil it is a vigorous grower and small plants should be spaced well away from it!

For very striking effect, *Phormium tenax*, known as the New Zealand flax, because of the value of its fibre, has great tough sword-like leaves almost 6 feet long. Standing up stiff and erect and colourful in blue-grey, this can dominate any low planting. Every few years a stout flowering panicle arises to some 8–10 feet with numerous exotic looking, 2-inch long, dull yellowish-red tubular flowers. It grows lustily even in sun and very sandy soil, but may be grown in some shade. A striking new addition to our family has been its variegated form, with leaves handsomely striped with yellow, and there is also a purple-leaved form if room can be found for it; this should be quite spectacular in effect.

Something of the same build is *Curtonus paniculatus*, a great montbretia with a massive sheaf of broad sword-like leaves, green but lax and arching and also very fine ground-cover. We like it mainly for its foliage, which gives variety, but the violent orange-red of its flowers is too blatant for us; however, their attribute of blooming late, in August and September, may be sufficient recommendation for many people.

A bold perennial not very often seen and one which can also do a good job of weed suppressing is *Buphthalmum speciosum*. At the streamside, or accommodating itself to any moist border, it puts up big, hairy, heart-shaped leaves which are handsome all through the summer and turn a cheerful golden-brown in the autumn. When the summer is well advanced and September on the way, *B. speciosum* will be showing large heads of orange-yellow, dark centred sunflowers on 3–4-foot stems. It is a robust growing plant, too strong growing for a small border, but very effective with clumps of bergenias or hostas as a foil for its massive appearance.

Another moisture lover and a large-leaved one is *Peltiphyllum peltatum* (*Saxifraga peltata*), the umbrella plant. It will also thrive at the streamside and where there is any area of really moist soil. In April it sends up strong, leafless rosy-tinted stems of 3 feet, topped with broad heads of many starry, pale pink flowers. After these are over, up come the large, perfectly rounded fresh green leaves, 6–8 inches across. When its annual cycle has been completed for the year and autumn calls, its dying shades of yellow are added to the season's colours.

The giant in the party is *Heracleum mantegazzianum*, a huge umbellifer from the Causasus; this immense plant towers up to 8–10 feet and is crested with a proportionately enormous head of white flowers, an inflorescence like cow parsley on the other end of Jodrell Bank telescope. Hardly a plant for a small garden, but for the wild places against a background of trees, or in an undulating garden one might contrive to look down upon it! It is monocarpic or biennial, but sows itself freely in the moistish sites which it likes.

Yet another slightly smaller giant is *Crambe cordifolia*, also from the Caucasus and like a monster gypsophila. In the background of a large border the crambe is ornamental in providing a large spreading cloud of daintiness, a crowd of sprays of small white flowers spreading out for several feet from its 6–7-foot stem.

A plant which always stands out in our memory is *Lavatera cachemirica* (syn. *L. cashmeriana*) which we once raised from seed from the annual distribution of the Royal Horticultural Society's seed. In the days when we were more 'border minded', this gave us a display throughout the summer and was a very long lived plant. Even then this took its place where the shrub border began and it came up to the height of a 6-foot shrub. Its satisfying patch of colour stood out for a long distance, its large rosy-pink flowers being like the more tender tree mallow, *L. olbia* 'Rosea'.

Turning once more to bolder plants, moisture lovers and woodlanders, the ligularias (senecios) fit into the wilder type of gardening. In a former garden where we began a taste for something more spectacular, we had *L. veitchiana* with enormous, rounded umbrella foliage. It makes a prominent feature by the waterside or the edge of woodland. Its tall 5-foot stems bear a plume of closely set, brilliant yellow flowers, an inspiring picture standing above the great leaves. As a substitute *L. wilsoniana* is equally impressive in any damp situation.

Another of these groundsels and better known is *L. clivorum* (known more correctly but less familiarly as *L. dentata*), a moisture lover which appreciates a little more sunshine. With substantial, heart-shaped leaves standing well clear of the ground, it sends up branching stems of 3 feet bearing large orange daisies in August. It provides colour between shrubs that have flowered earlier and shows up well against them. Plenty of space should be allowed as it is a vigorous grower when suited. The cultivar *L. clivorum*

'Desdemona' is a first-class 'colour foliage' plant with purple leaves, dark purple stems and large flower heads of orange-yellow. Not so robust as the former, it is most effective standing on its own among primulas.

The giant rhubarb, *Rheum palmatum*, is also a memory from another garden, where for lack of room it grew at the side of the compost heap and showed its appreciation of its generally rich soil and moist surroundings by putting up leaves of tropical magnificence. When growing up to flower it used to be an annual marvel, so rapid was it that one could almost see it grow, but then, 8–10 feet is a long way to go. Finally, it ends up with panicles of creamy-white flowers. Put in rich moist soil in woodland or by the streamside, it is a stately spectacle. There are a few more fine subjects that might be explored in this family, and we were pleased to find a new and smaller one which is easy to fit into a small border. It is R. *kialense* from China, and this has comparatively small, heart-shaped leaves and sends up branching, 2-foot stems which are packed with blush-pink flowers in May.

Verbascums come among these stately growers and are best isolated from too many plants around them. The taller ones, with spikes that average 4–6 feet, are easily satisfied as to soil and give a long display from June to September, with a range of colour to suit all tastes. Apart from the lovely named hybrids such as 'Gainsborough' primrose-yellow, 'Pink Domino' mauve-pink, and 'Cotswold Queen' salmon-bronze, there are many other good art shades. Quite a few verbascums are biennial, but have a happy habit of returning again from self-sown seedlings.

For those who enjoy the fascination of raising a few things from seed, these verbascums can be exciting and come along quickly and often flower within a year. A look through a specialist seed catalogue will show various species, all alluring and wonderfully described. *V.* 'Miss Wilmott' came to us like this, and has been no disappointment, but a fine 4–5-foot plant with large, pure white flowers, re-seeding itself true but for the exception of an occasional yellow. Another lucky dip was *V. chaixii* 'Alba', a graceful 4–5 feet with white flowers and dark coloured stamens. Grey-green leaves distinguish *V. vernale*, a good perennial which flowers in July with a strong 5–6-foot architectural form. Most of

Tricyrtis macropoda. The earliest of the Toad-lilies to flower

J. R. A. Davies

Sisyrinchium striatum

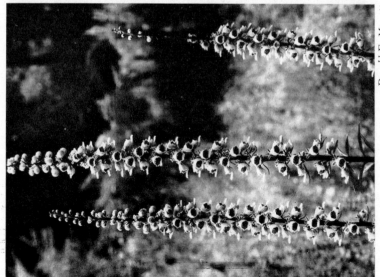

Donald F. Merrett

Digitalis ferruginea

Rogersia in woodland setting

H. E. Bawden

Euphorbia mellifera with rhododendron-like foliage

H. E. Bawden

Phormium tenax

J. R. A. Davies

Iris pallida 'variegata'

Helichrysum fontanesii. Enjoying the sun on sandy slopes

J. R. A. Davies

Hieracium bombycinum. An aristocrat among the grey-foliaged plants

H. E. Bawden

Miscanthus sinensis '*Variegatus*' of architectural value
for focal points

these verbascums stand up well, but nature loves her pranks at times, little whirlwinds, hefty huffs and just one more puff to show who really is the master. To save reproaches and having them twisted and made unsightly by the wind, a thin cane 3–4 feet high, placed behind and close to the spike, a few neat ties that are hardly noticed, and your insurance is paid.

Irises can also come into the composition of the picture, mostly so in summer time when their grassy foliage gently waves above other plants. There is no denying that the flowers have a classical beauty, though on the whole theirs is a fleeting display. There is one we would always choose as fitting to be with any selection, and that is *Iris ochroleuca*. It has strong, spear-like leaves growing up to 3–4 feet, a flowering spike rising to 5 feet, and beautifully formed blossoms of creamy-white in July, often continuing to flower later. If you are lucky enough to have a stream, what is more suitable and natural a plant for the English garden than our own native *I. pseudacorus*, relishing the waterside with close clumps of 4-foot waving greenery and yellow flags!

To our regret, our present garden does not contain any of the very ornamental eremurus, a thing that has to be remedied, for they are of unparalleled beauty and the noblest of the liliaceous family. Grouping them between shrubs and in warm borders or sheltered parts of open woodland, their tall and beautiful flowering spires show up to perfection. Unfortunately, they are slow growing, expensive to buy and not very easy to obtain. Their main requirements are a good, deep, rich soil and sunshine. We lost the few that we moved here because their chosen site turned out to be wetter than we thought it might be—good drainage is a very important factor in their cultivation.

One thing we have always tried to do is to have plants to give interest and bloom in the later summer and autumn. Some of the aconitums fill this role for the mixed border and are particularly suitable for growing among shrubs. A number open their flowers in late August and September when so many plants are on the wane, and then they continue into October. Though these monkshoods are old-timers, and so closely related to the delphiniums, they are comparatively rare in gardens, in spite of the fact that they are easily grown and do well in semi-shade as well as sun. We always find their blue-hooded flowers rather intriguing, and their deeply cut foliage attractive all the season, as well as their being ornamental when boldly grouped. It must be admitted, however, that all parts of the plant are very poisonous.

Aconitum wilsonii is one of the finest, being at its best in October, and rising prominently to 5–6 feet or more with good-sized flowers of rich violet-blue. Most of the monkshoods are in varying shades of darkish blues, but *A. lycoctonum* gives a lighter effect with pale yellow flowers in July and August, and a height of 3 feet. A newer one, 'Bressingham Spire', which is a cultivar of *A. napellus*, comes into the picture in July and August, rising to 3 feet. It has an exceptionally fine, branching and long tapering spire of violet-blue.

Lobelia cardinalis affords another example of a tall plant that can be used in a telling manner to make an arresting splash of colour which stands out for a long distance. Of course, its brilliant vivid scarlet needs careful placing, but so free flowering a plant should not be overlooked, and its purple coloured foliage is an asset. Moist soil near the waterside is its natural home, and there is something to be said for that, for one associates water with a green sward around it, a good background for this difficult colour. However, with some thought it may be well placed in the wetter part of the border. Though we have not had great success in keeping it long, it can be so, even somewhat disconcerting when gardening friends point nonchalantly to an obviously old clump and say: 'Oh, they have been there almost ten years.'

One of the tallest and most effective of the artemisias is *A. lactiflora*, which makes 4–5 feet or more. It is magnificent in July when its stout stems carry spiraea-like plumes composed of many small, milk-white flowers which continue to be in the picture for a long time. Unlike most of the family, which is rich in silver and grey-leaved plants, these are green and deeply cut, though silver backed. It also has a preference for moister soil and, besides the border, it may be impressive isolated in part shade or thin woodland.

Also architectural in a minor way, and always interesting for its bluish-green leaves, is the caper spurge, *Euphorbia lathyrus*. Though it is a biennial, it has a habit of sowing itself freely. Since it is a stiff erect grower and only foliaged with well spaced opposite leaves it does little harm among any plants and blooms in its second year at 1½–2 feet, giving greenish flowers. It is said to have mole-repelling qualities and, though we have never grown it for this purpose, it may well be that a quantity of this euphorbia grown in the garden would be effective.

Quite a number of these spurges are majestic plants to build around, and a challenge to one's artistic talents. *E. characias*, with shrubby stems and glaucous-green foliage, is really a most imposing sight when seen as a large clump 3–4 feet high and in full flower, with huge heads of greenish-yellow, brown-spotted flowers, which last for months from early spring. *E. wulfenii* also forms many-stemmed clumps over 3 feet tall, well foliaged in glaucous-green. It bears large, rounded heads of pale greeny-yellow, accentuated with black, which seem unending from spring onwards. An undercarpet of lowly plants such as *Alchemilla mollis*, the bergenias, hostas and so on, are good for emphasizing such prominent features as these spurges. All are sun-lovers, appreciating the drier and warm parts of the garden; some of the best specimens we have seen have been nestling against large established conifers.

If you have a warm or sheltered corner, try and acquire *E. mellifera*; it is particularly lovely, the foliage soft green and prominently marked with a light band down the centre. In its full growth in mid-summer, its magnificent, broad leaves can be as long as 8–10 inches and almost rhododendron-like in appearance. About 3 feet high, it has honey-scented, green and yellow flowers, centred with black, which are produced on the previous year's growth. Though the tops were killed in the 1962–63 winter, it sprang to life in the later summer and is now a robust plant again.

Euphorbia griffithii is deciduous but is an early riser, showing up by February, and by late April, at 10–12 inches tall, is already showing a turn of colour with reddish shoots with a lively chequering of light and bright green displayed upon them. That is its first stage of beauty, then, quite rapidly it reaches 3 feet to give arresting heads of burnt orange. In its early weeks there is little to quarrel with its colour, but as it lasts well into July, it is best in part shade among evergreen shrubs. It spreads by stolons, forming ever widening thickets and is almost too happy in our soil—after seven to eight years we have to have a war upon it now and then. For all that, it is a magnificent plant and everybody must have a piece!

Add to these *E. sikkimensis*, and one has a representative collection of the best of the taller ones for spectacular planting. *Sikkimensis* is especially exciting in the early spring with its new leaves and stems a glowing ruby-red, later turning to soft green as they grow to over 3 feet. The pale yellow, flat heads of flowers come later than most and tone well with the shrubs and almost any border plants. Though not so forceful as *griffithii*, it has the same running habit, but when necessary and when it has wandered too far, it is amenable to being collected in the spring, and its shoots thrust more compactly together to make a good solid clump.

The rodgersias qualify in these notes by reason of their superb foliage and tall panicles of flower. With the exception of *tabularis* they are not for gardens of limited space. Though not liking boggy soil, they are good subjects to grow near the waterside, for their luxuriant appearance is in harmony with the peaceful surroundings. They belong to the vast saxifrage family and, like so many of these, bear hundreds of small flowers which give daintiness to their floral effect. *Rodgersia tabularis* can be recommended as it does not make great demands upon space, and could well be chosen as a single attractive feature for a small garden. The perfectly rounded, soft green leaves, more than 18 inches across, are beautiful to look upon, and from among them rise the 3–4-foot flowering stems. The flowers are borne in June, an astilbe-like plume in creamy-white. *R. podophylla* is very distinct and one of the oldest in cultivation, yet not often seen. It is one of the most colourful in foliage, shining metallic-bronze in the sunshine and very deeply cut—a picturesque plant with its yellowish-white flowers on 3-foot stalks in June. *R. aesculifolia*, with great horse-chestnut foliage, very conspicuously hairy, is more often seen. It is one of the tallest, sending up a strong 4–5-foot stem with an arching panicle of hundreds of small white flowers which remain for a long time, then gradually fade to pink. Another beautiful species, *R. pinnata* with handsome dark green leaves, has panicles of pink flowers and attains 2–3 feet. All these assume handsome foliage colour in the autumn.

At one time the kniphofias were regarded as giving the most effective colour for the autumn border, but now many good hybrids have a range from June to October. It is as well to bear in mind that their country of origin is South Africa, and they are sun-lovers, the better for warm sandy soil, rather than a cold one. It is their stately spikes of colourful flowers that have earned them the worthy title of Torch Lilies. The old *K.* 'Royal Standard' is still one of the best and hardiest, striking in its crimson and gold in July and August, to a height of 3–4 feet. *K. corallina* goes up to 3 feet with soft red flowers, a reliable variety. The very hardy *K. caulescens* is quite outstanding, with its wonderful glaucous-blue foliage and great stems to over 4 feet, bearing reddish-salmon flowers which fade off to almost white. 'Maid of Orleans' is a beautiful colour break, with ivory-white flowers from July to September. There are many more to choose from, but two smaller, late flowering species, *K. galpinii* and *K. rufa*, are worth a special sunny place. *Galpinii* is a dainty dwarf with grass-like leaves and soft orange-scarlet flowers on 18-inch stems. *K. rufa* has slender pokers of yellow flowers in July and grows up to 2 feet.

An old-fashioned plant that we used to grow and like is *Macleaya cordata* (syn. *Bocconia yedoensis*) known as the plume poppy, though not on account of its flower shape. It is a 6-foot, stately plant, which in spite of its height rarely needs staking, especially if grown between shrubs. Handsome, rounded, exquisitely lobed grey-green leaves, alternatively placed up the tall glaucous stems, are a distinct feature. To complete the picture, in July the branching spire is decorated with a cloud of buff, starry flowers. It is an easy and robust grower, a plant of much architectural quality.

A grand plant that might tend to be overlooked in a desire for colour only, could be the old plant of herb gardens, *Angelica archangelica*, a giant umbellifer. It dies when it flowers, but you may enjoy its luxuriant, bright green foliage for two to three years before this happens. Then one year it will send up a stout stem for its swan song, and seeds to provide future progeny. It may be 4, 5, or 6 feet high, according to your soil, and it will bear wide, rounded umbels of greenish-white flowers, the effect in all being like a huge cow parsley. Not very exciting, you might think, but cow parsley has a wonderful make-up when observed closely in a vase with coloured flowers to complement it. It is decorative in seed and sows itself freely. Having seen what it can do, it is easier to decide just where to leave or to transplant the seedlings, for two or three may be quite enough! On its own, uncluttered by other plants, it is in its full grandeur.

Of the same family are the fennels (*Ferula*), but very different in appearance, having very graceful finely divided, hair-like leaves of the freshest green, at their best in the early spring. *Ferula communis* throws up shoots of 5–6 feet with heads of greenish-yellow. *F. communis* 'Purpurea' gives variety with foliage of brownish-purple. Another of these striking *Umbelliferae*, which we think eclipses them all, is *Selinum carvifolia* (syn. *S. tenuifolium*). It has the filmiest of ferny leaves of an exquisite green. In the late summer it bears branching, triangular umbels of white flowers, so refined as to give the effect of a dainty, inverted, white-laced parasol in appearance. It grows up to 6–7 feet.

Writing about plants reminds us of a number raised from seed in our earlier days. Woad (*Isatis tinctoria*) caught our imagination to have a glimpse back into time, for it dates back into our earlier history when Caesar came to find the Britons (so history says) stained blue with it—or was it the cold? Even in the Middle Ages this was still used extensively as a dye and was quite a thriving industry. The plant is biennial, shooting up to 3 feet by early May, and branching out with multitudes of small yellow flowers for a good many weeks. In a border there is little to compete with its height at that time and it can look too isolated, but among shrubs or with a background such as climbing roses it can be picturesque. Plenty of shiny black seeds are formed, and often self-sown seedlings will tower up much higher.

The autumn months are always pleasant ones, the haste of the spring and doing jobs to time are over, the grass needs less mowing; a time of more leisure has come. Now the shrubs are in berry, but the unusual *Phytolacca americana* competes with some of them in its tall bearing, autumn leaf and stem colouring of reddish-purple, and trusses of purple-black berries. It is an interesting perennial, standing up to almost 5 feet, with racemes of small, creamy-white flowers contrasting with broad dark green leaves. Its appearance gives the impression of liking the steamy, swampy forest, we do not know if this is in fact the case, but at least it enjoys fairly moist soil and is an effective foliage plant where the garden merges into woodland. Other occupants that fit into such an environment or the moist end of the border are the cimicifugas which can also be reckoned with these late summer pleasures. There are a number of these with which to become acquainted, all valuable for erect growth, ferny leaves and long fluffy plumes of white to creamy-white flowers. *Cimicifuga racemosa* and *C. simplex* both grace the late autumn with slender spires of 4–5 feet, elegant and refined. They are easily grown and when settled down will send up numerous close spikes which take up little room.

As far as really stately plants are concerned, there are few that compare with the onopordons to create an astonishing point of interest in the background of a border. They are effective mainly for their large, tropical looking leaves, with a silvery-white down upon them, rather than their branching heads of mauve, thistle-like flowers. *Onopordon acanthium*, known as the Scotch thistle, rises up to 6–7 feet, and *O. arabicum* up to 8–10 feet. Both are biennials which thrive in any sunny position and will sow themselves. Before our mechanical age, the old-timer, the biennial Fuller's teasel (*Dipsacus fullonum*) was of industrial value, the bristly heads being used for brushing the nap on certain kinds of material. We have had this appear in the garden, the first year showing a verbascum-like rosette. Its second year brings a 5-foot stem with a flower of little consequence, but which forms an ornamental bristly head. If dried and dipped in silver, gold or other paint, it is excellent for winter decoration.

Dicentra spectabilis is the king of the dicentras, an architectural plant in a smaller way. Flowering in April when there are few plants of its height, it needs to be between shrubs so that it does not appear too lonely and isolated. Shrubs also give it a measure of protection from spring frosts. The best plant we ever saw, bearing a dozen or more 2-foot spikes, was on the shady side of a house wall. It was *D. spectabilis* at its best, a unique and beautiful plant, its rosy-red, white-tipped flowers hanging gracefully from pendulous stems. The pendant, heart-shaped flowers of this fine old plant have earned it the names of 'ladies' locket', 'bleeding heart' and 'lady-in-the-bath', 'Dutchman's breeches' and other titles of loving esteem.

Though the Cape hyacinth, *Galtonia candicans*, is a bulbous plant, we think it worthy of a place among these of noble stature. Considering the cheapness of the bulbs and its value as a late flowerer it is worthy of more appreciation. In a good soil, which it enjoys, it will be seen at its best, towering gracefully up to 4-5 feet; in August its thick stems will be hung with tiers of great, snow-white bells which continue to open week after week. A group looks imposing above the foliage of irises, or rising up above medium-sized shrubs where they are more protected from wind. Grown in full sun its stem is usually strong enough not to need support, but a wind in a frolic can distort the beauty of its spike and it is a wise precaution to stake it carefully with a thin cane. The bulbs should be planted 5-6 inches deep, and in early March, to give them a chance to get a good roothold.

A plant which might well be used more for its imposing appearance in the border is the giant knapweed, *Centurea macrocephala*. It sends up stout stems of 4-5 feet which are crowned with bold, thistle-like heads in June and July. These are bright yellow globes which may be as much as 3-4 inches across and, with the embellishment of a papery calyx surrounding each, much is added to its attraction. It is robust and easily grown and looks best as an individual plant.

Having such a wealth of native ferns furnishing the garden and around us, we have learned to appreciate their beauty, varied greens and loveliness of texture. One we have always found desirable is *Polystichum setigerum*, the soft shield fern. It will form a great circular mound, which is a thing of beauty all the year. Old plants will pile up to over 2 feet and be a background feature in shady woodland, and with groups of glaucous leaved hostas in the foreground, the picture for the summer is completed. A hardy fern which we can also recommend is *Matteuccia struthiopteris*, the graceful ostrich fern of such statuesque appearance for moist shady borders or waterside. It stands stiffly erect up to 3 feet, its dainty fronds spaced regularly along the plume, which is very beautiful as the pale green fronds arise from the ground in late spring; it is a strong grower and makes good cover in woodland.

Most of the sisyrinchiums are dwarf plants, but a Triton among the minnows is *Sisyrinchium striatum*, a robust plant with sword-like, glaucous-green foliage. Though these sisyrinchiums may seed about almost too freely, at least they have the blessing of being evergreen, and *striatum* is of architectural value in the winter. In June it puts forth sturdy, 2-foot stems which bear a multitude of pale yellow flowers for a long period. It comes from the Chilean Andes, and is perfectly hardy in full sun and sandy soil.

Even in the smallest plot, corner of the rock garden or alpine lawn, just one plant can be the making of the picture, and become a miniature architectural feature. Though it may not last overlong in flower, the erect-growing *Veronica gentianoides*, towering over an inch-high carpet of plants can dramatize the scene, as will a small group of *Verbascum phoeniceum*. For a longer flowering time the compact-growing *Calamintha nepetoides* can put on its modest show to dominate small carpeting plants. For an exotic sub-tropical look, the incarvilleas give their pageant with a flourish of rosy trumpets, or the gaudy tigridias can 'strut their hour upon the stage'. Over low groupings of violas, *Penstemon campanulatus* 'Evelyn', nicely erect and compact, can be more soothing in its softer colouring. Grassy foliage has great value, Bowles's Golden Grass giving an all-season feature in golden-yellow, and to add but one more, the evergreen *Diplarrhena moraea* of orchis-like display.

✻ 7 ✻

Silver and Grey, Variegated Foliage, and Grasses

THERE IS NO doubt that flower arranging has done much to educate us in the appreciation of the beauty of leaf forms from handsome boldness to delicate refinement, in all the subtle variations of leaf colour and, above all, on the varied uses of silver and grey foliage plants. The old herbaceous border tended to be such a mass of colour that nothing was clearly distinguishable—almost meaningless! The great thing about these silvery-foliaged plants is that, besides giving distinction and providing contrast, they mix well with almost any bright colours. Shrubby plants such as santolinas, *Senecio greyi*, *Ruta* 'Jackman's Blue', *Phlomis fruticosa*, and *Helichrysum trilineatum* (syn. *H. splendidum*, *H. aveolatum*) are all valuable and give their own show of flower, but there is a good selection of herbaceous material to choose from as well.

Hardly anything stands out so prominently in a front row planting as *Senecio cineraria* (syn. *Cineraria maritima*) with its lovely mass of drooping, serrated silvery-grey leaves. In our dryish soil this has wintered through all seasons, even 1962–63, but this is not so in all gardens and it must be where it is pretty sharply drained to survive many years. A much hardier cultivar is *S. maritima* 'White Diamond', interesting at all times and with a very powdery whiteness of leaf. Old foliage can be cut away in the spring and the result will be much more new growth of silvery whiteness. Rather like these senecios in leaf is *Artemisia stelleriana*, another very silvery-white, show plant for a warm dry place. With a robust, prostrate habit it is most striking when hanging down from a wall or in a large paving pocket. There are a number of these artemisia species which give a light touch in feathery, bushy plants and range over a foot or so in height. In this class are *A. nutans*, *A. palmeri* and *A. valesiaca*, all about 18 inches and useful for contrast near the foreground. A low bushy one is *A. canescens*, giving foot-wide cover of silvery, very finely cut foliage. The flowers of these artemisias are usually small and uninteresting, but their decorative silver foliage mingles and tones so well with other colourful plants. It must be observed that most of them are drought resisting and appreciate sun, good drainage and warm soil. They can be cut back to within 5–6 inches in the spring.

Almost indestructible is *Anthemis cupaniana*, one of the best and easiest of low-growing silvers, which forms a wide mat of dissected foliage, and gives a long succession of large white daisies. Another easy going mat-forming plant which is seldom seen is *Eriophyllum lanatum*. Given a well drained place with plenty of elbow room, it forms a good foliage mass of silvery-grey, well matched with cheerful, orange-yellow daisy flowers.

An important group of plants are the anaphalis, valuable not only for their grey foliage but for their branching heads of fluffy little white everlasting flowers. Most of them enjoy full sun and one of our great favourites is *A. triplinervis* which prefers moister soil and does well with a modicum of shade. Unlike the other two, it is a stay-at-home compact plant and, having broad, flat rosettes of gleaming silvery whiteness, it is ideal for the edge of plantings. It flowers in July and right away into the autumn, and its 10–12-inch stems bear white flowers with a dark centre, which adds to its attraction. It is most effective in clumps and a good ground-covering plant; easily divided to obtain more plants. *A. margaritacea* and *A. yedoense*, silvery, but smaller in leaf, are erect growers up to 18–20 inches and do not need staking. They are of more spreading habit and have masses of white, fluffy heads which last exceptionally well when cut for decoration. Both of these are easy plants and spread well but are not invasive.

Some of the chrysanthemums are excellent grey foliaged plants, the 2-foot *Chrysanthemum parthenium* 'Plenum' being useful at mid-border, and its double white neat daisies are good for cutting. In sharply drained soil *C. densum amanum* (syn. *Tanacetum densum*

'Amani', *C. haradjanii*) may be used as a low-edging plant, for it forms the most delightful mounds of finely cut silvery leaves which are topped with quite large white flowers.

Other low-edging plants are some of the achilleas. Though more of a rock garden plant, *Achillea kellereri* is an attractive one and does well in a warm border. It makes low foot-wide tufts of long, narrow, finely cut leaves, very silvery-white and with clusters of short stemmed white flowers. *A. argentea* is also a mat forming carpet of silver, with short heads of white flowers. *A. clavenae* is similarly mat forming and silvery. One of the showiest is *A. clypeolata*, with very much larger leaves than *kellereri*, which forms a big dome of silvery fern-like foliage covered with flat heads of golden-yellow daisies in July.

Apart from the shrubby *Helichrysum rosmarinifolium* 'Purpurascens' all the helichrysums we know are of silver and grey in a variety of intenseness, from the little rock garden *H. bellidioides* to the 3-foot bushes of *H. trilineatum*. The latter is adaptable to any sunny mixed border, as it can be cut back fairly hard to produce compactness and gives an extra silvery quality when it breaks into new growth. It is very hardy and in its summer glory its woolly, silvery leaves are very ornamental; these also help to light up the winter scene. Since its first blossoms of old gold begin in May and are still aglow in November, it gives very good value, besides being good as a cut flower. *H. bellidioides* claims a place here for the value of its silvery-green carpet, its hearty constitution in sunny places or paving pockets, and its mass of little white-papery flowers. *H. fontanesii* is outstanding for a sunny bed where special and unique plants may be gathered together. It forms semi-shrubby, foot high, wide bushes with a mass of very narrow, intensely silvery-white leaves and has sprays of yellow flower heads much like the old Curry Plant, *H. angustifolium*. It may not look as though it would survive our damp, wet, fog and lumps of snow, but it is quite hardy. It is a lovely foil to clumps of the pasque flower (*Pulsatilla vulgaris*), when their beautiful violet and purple cups herald so many more good things to come.

Helichrysum petiolatum is not hardy, though it will get by on the occasions that we have a mild winter. It is a splendid space filler for hot, dry places however, and from a small plant put out in

April or May its semi-prostrate growths will have formed a 2–3 foot network of silvery-grey by the end of the summer. It is also excellent for paving or ornamental tubs and garden vases, and fine for flower arrangement. Another first-class silver plant which has to be regarded as tender is *Centaurea gymnocarpa*, so often used in bedding out and a perfect foil to high colours such as the spectacular cannas. Its mass of long, pinnate foliage builds up into a wonderful mound of silvery-grey. *Senecio leucostachys* is yet another with deeply cut elegant foliage; in sheltered positions it will sometimes come through if the winter is not too severe. With greenhouse facilities these three can easily be maintained from cuttings.

The silvery-leaved thymes also come into the garden make-up in filling modest corners, and give scent and colour too. They are evergreys that add to the winter furnishing, and all they need is the drier sunnier positions that remind them of their warmer homelands. The silvery, minute foliaged *Thymus nitidus* is perhaps the best known of these, a little 12-inch bushlet, Lilliputian and aromatic. June brings forth its cloud of pale rosy-lilac flowers which the bees love so much. Even more silvery-leaved is the highly aromatic *T. mastichina* which likes a specially warm place. It is a miniature 12–15-inch bush, also flowering in June, when it is covered with heads of creamy-white flowers which are followed by a foam of fluffy seed heads. For the flat pockets in the paving there are *T. lanuginosus* and *T. doefleri*, which will grow rapidly into inch-high carpets of grey woolliness.

Along with these smaller shrubby furnishings for the sun borders, one of the least common of the lavenders, *Lavandula lanata*, might be grown for its neat low hump of soft, woolly grey leaves. Above these in July 12-inch heads of dark blue blossoms continue into September, having the same delicious fragrance as the other lavenders. All these shrubby lavenders are important and, though the purpose of these notes is to deal with the plants to mingle and mix with shrubs, this is just a reminder of their great value for grey effect. Also *Ruta* 'Jackman's Blue' must be kept in mind for its striking blue foliage and compact habit.

The merits of the eryngiums often seem to be overlooked, yet their silvery-grey foliage and steely-blue, thistle-like heads can be an admirable foil to other plants as well as exceedingly ornamental on their own. As a small specimen plant, *Eryngium bourgatii* has distinction in its very silvery, deeply cut and lightly veined foliage. Scarcely more than a foot in height, its group of branching heads of steely-blue flowers last from June almost into August. We were given this plant with due warning that it would spread, but so far its rosette of leaves keeps reasonably compact, and that after quite a few years. One of the most beautiful is *E. alpinum* which differs with a basal tuft of heart-shaped leaves, but both its 2-foot stems and flowers are a wonderful soft steely-blue and long-lasting. The taller *E. oliverianum* is better known as a mid-border plant and useful as a July-September flowerer. It is outstanding in quality and decorative effect, standing stiffly erect at 3 feet, with flowers and stems of a bright metallic blue, almost as though the colouring had been painted on. One of the most exciting and startling in appearance is *E. giganteum*, sometimes referred to as 'Miss Wilmott's Ghost'. Not to worry! It is only in the dimmish evening light that the very silvery-white bracts surrounding the flower heads, might appear spectre-like. Above the bracts it carries a large, ornamental, teasel-like head of pale blue, which lasts for a long time and, like all of them, may be cut and dried for winter decoration; it is a biennial but will sow itself. Though it is often given as 3–4 feet in height, we have not had it over 2 feet in any soil. *E. variifolium* is worth growing more for its marbled, white-veined, evergreen foliage than for its flowers which are not so striking. All of these thrive in sandy soil and sun.

Quite a good plant to sprawl at the foot of the taller eryngiums is *Glaucium flavum*, the horned poppy of our coasts, and this also thrives in sandy soil and sun. It may be short lived but can be perennial in sandy soil, though is usually treated as an annual, and can be obliging in producing self-sowns. Close-planted in a group, the bold, deeply cut, silvery-white leaves are highly ornamental, and the yellow flowers are almost 3 inches across and held on 2-foot stems, giving a brilliant display from June onwards. If grown as an annual it should be sown in March.

Though some of the hawkweeds are spreaders and must be used with discretion, one which is always admired for its foliage is *Hieraceum bombycinum*. It is non-ramping, forming a rosette of many 6–8-inch-long leaves like white plush. The beauty of the silvery, blue-grey, woolly leaves is quite breathtaking when the early morning sun plays softly upon them. Its yellow daisy flowers are weedy and of no artistic value, but will serve to produce self-sown seedlings in due course. It starts into leaf in late spring and any sunny, well drained position will suit it.

Another of our favourites of exceptional foliage value is *Marrubium candidissimum*, which forms a dwarf spreading mass some 18 inches across. It is thickly foliaged with rounded felt-like leaves of soft sage-green, the growths being velvety and silver stemmed. It is especially delightful when rain drops glisten upon it. Coming from the Mediterranean, it likes sun and poor soil. It is a labiate, a botanist's puzzle and delight, and has an array of aliases such as *M. cylleaneum*, *M. velutinum*, or it might even be found under another genus such as *Ballota* or *Sideritis*. The whorls of very pale lilac flowers are of little ornament.

The low growing, silvery carpeting plants include *Veronica incana*, *V. pectinata* 'Rosea' and *Antennaria dioica*. *Veronica incana* is outstanding with its prostrate mat of fairly large, ashen-grey leaves. In June and July its foot high, upright, rich violet-blue spikes contrast beautifully with its foliage; it does best in well drained sandy soil. *V. pectinata* 'Rosea' is a carpeter for the rock garden, paving, or sandy sunny places where it will form a prostrate mass of grey-green toothed leaves and short sprays of pink flowers in May and June. *Antennaria dioica* will clothe paving pockets and light up the side of gravel paths with a close, creeping patchwork of intensely silvery-white foliage, sending up short spikes with heads of long-lasting, pink flowers in summer. Then there is one of the labiates, *Teucrium orientale*, a dwarf creeping plant that can be recommended for its cushions of silvery-grey and intriguing heads of pale yellow flowers. Presuming this to be one of the Mediterranean clan, we planted it in a warm place. Though it looks a bit lifeless in winter time, it soon responds to the effect of warmer days. The very dwarf *Artemisia schmidtii* 'Nana' also behaves like this before it springs to life again, and then it forms a foot-wide carpet of astonishing beauty with the silkiest of finely cut silvery leaves. It makes a good groundwork against other dark and small mat-forming plants, such as the dark green *Achillea tomentosa*.

The silver and grey of some of the acaenas form wonderful sheets of foliage, but have to be used with discretion and kept away from other plants. They are best confined to paving pockets, and for us their creeping woody stems help to bind and hold sandy pathways. Such is the prostrate silvery-green of *Acaena buchananii*, which forms a ferny-leaved carpet. Two which rarely escape notice in the garden are *A. adscendens* and *A. glauca*. These differ in being strong growing, trailing plants, sending out long stems from a central rootstock. *A. adscendens* has very steely-blue rosaceous foliage, and by mid-summer has rounded ornamental seed heads of coppery-bronze. The rarer *A. glauca* is singularly beautiful in leaf, very blue, enhanced with reddish stems. Both of these will cover well over 2 feet of space and, being evergreen, are worth a conspicuous place for winter ornament. Both look well in walls, trailing from the top or even as ground-cover under roses. They may be trimmed back to shape when necessary.

Variegated Plants

One of the first plants that came our way among the variegated fraternity of plants was *Mentha rotundifolia* 'Variegata', and we think it one of the handsomest. A combination of pale green leaves and soft gold around the edge of the foliage endows it with a striking beauty that is permanent during its summer growth. Like most mints it will rapidly carpet the ground. Equally striking, and generally admired by all, is *Scrophularia aquatica* 'Variegata'. It does not aspire to any beauty of flower, but with its green foliage clearly margined and splashed with creamy-white, it claims immediate attention, especially if in contrast to darker foliage. Nature's work of bestowing variegation upon this plant has beautified it immeasurably. Apart from its height of 3 feet, stiff erect habit and square stems of the wild plant, it is almost unrecognizable as a form of it. Some say shade for this, but with us it does best in sunshine where it is fairly moist.

Of *Lamium galeobdolon* 'Variegatum' one might say that it gambols, for it obliges by covering yards as ground-cover around shrubs and trees in shade and any other sunless spot that is better covered with an evergreen. The pale yellow, upstanding heads of

flowers come in the spring, but its carpet of silvery variegation is
its greatest asset and very much more noticeable in winter time.
Then the silveriness is intensified to a greater degree.

Though by no means one of the highbrow plants, *L. maculatum*
is indispensable as a carpeter. After its early and very colourful
mass of rosy-purple flowers, the white-striped variegated leaves
are much in evidence for the rest of the year. It will naturalize in
sun or part shade, but flowers more freely in full sun and poor
soil. Besides the rosy-purple kind, there are many worth while and
charming intermediate forms to look for, pinks and delicate pale
pinks, some less rampageous, and good clear whites. *L. m.*
'Aureum' is outstanding as a colour-foliage plant with its striking
golden leaves. It provides a satisfying low mat which is compli-
mentary to taller plants or those with darker leaves. It is not a
strong grower and needs occasional division to keep it growing
healthily and it likes shade and moist soil. Also brilliantly yellow
in foliage is the yellow form of creeping jenny, *Lysimachia nummularia* 'Aurea', a perfectly flat-growing little ramper that forms a
very decorative pattern at the foot of any chosen shrub.

A group of the variegated irises can be a very striking picture
and all help with the window dressing, for their grassy leaves
stand up prominently. In the summer time *Iris pallida* 'Variegata'
is one of the most outstanding, with its band of golden variegation
on the 1½–2-foot high leaves. A good clump of this is very beautiful, especially when isolated from taller plants. It is a fairly vigorous
grower and divisions can soon be made to widen a clump. Besides
its colour-foliage value, its 3-foot stems bear very lovely, light
lavender flowers which come out in May. There is also the silver
variegated form which can be just as striking a feature for landscape effect.

The variegated cultivar of *I. foetidissima* has the advantage over
the last two in being evergreen. It is picturesque with cream-
striped leaves which are every bit as good in winter time. Then,
our other native plant *I. pseudacorus*, the moisture lover, with its
compact clump of 3–4-foot leafage, also gives a striking cultivar
with creamy-yellow stripes. It is most noticeable in the early
spring months, but they turn green towards the end of the
summer. Another one to draw the eye and make a low, spreading

colourful cover is *I. japonica* 'Variegata' with white bands down
the centre of the leaves. Having found this none too pleased in a
severe winter, it now thrives in a warmer, moist position.

Verbascum bombyciferum is always in fashion for its architectural
value in sky-scraping, sometimes well over 8 feet, and notably a
must for its large rosettes of silvery, woolly leaves which will
cover a good 2 feet of space. A picture on its own, for even the
great flowering spike is covered with silvery wool. When, in June
and July, the tall branching stem is fully adorned with pale yellow
flowers, it is spectacular. It is biennial but seeds itself; usually it
does not need staking.

To these erect and spire-shaped plants may be added *Perovskia
atriplicifolia*, known as the Russian sage. Apart from its flowers,
the greyish stems of its wand-like growths are exceedingly handsome and should not be obscured by close planting. In spite of its
height of 3–4 feet, it can be very effective almost to the fore of a
border. Late flowering is another of its assets and its slender spires
and branchlets will be covered with a cloud of pale violet flowers
from August to September. Perovskia likes its warm, well drained
position and should be pruned back to 3–4 inches in the spring.
Fortunately its stems are so strong that staking may be forgotten.
Physostegia 'Vivid' which will also be in bloom at the same time,
is a fine companion to it.

A pleasant surprise among the ornamental silvers has been *Leucanthemum hosmariense* which we first grew in the rock garden.
Coming from the mountains of Morocco, we viewed it with due
suspicion, but it has proved perfectly hardy. Furthermore, a few
spare plants were tried in a very dry position where our losses had
been legion. In spite of this place of ruin, it seems at its best, and
thrives on past dead bodies. It forms a most attractive 12-inch
dome of finely cut, silvery-grey leaves, and remains so throughout
the year. Though it often has a few flowers out as late as December, its main period is June to July when its white, 2-inch wide
yellow-eyed daises are held nicely up for viewing.

Grasses

We have only to look at the great flowering plumes of pampas grass, *Cortaderia selloana* (syn. *C. argentea*), to realize how impressive grasses can be in the garden. While we do not profess to know this vast family, we have become more conscious of their use as background, contrast and colour value besides their use as floral decoration. Among them are distinct colourings of yellow, rich green, blues and striking variegations, combined with an unusual and graceful beauty of flower. They are divided between annual species, such as *Briza maxima*, and deciduous and evergreen perennials.

Though annual, *Briza maxima*, the quaking grass, is always somewhere in the garden, clutches of its bluish-green foliage soon replacing its lost parent. At flowering time its papery heads swing elegantly, it looks precariously, yet surprisingly strongly held, on the frailest of wiry stems. *Phalaris arundinacea* 'Picta', long known in gardens as gardener's garters, is a variegated form of our own native plant; it is conspicuous for its white-striped leaves, which make a good contrast against other plants in the border. In some soils it may spread too rapidly, but it may be divided. It grows to 2–2½ feet high but is not evergreen.

Evergreen and silvery-blue in foliage is *Avena sempervirens*, easily one of our favourites for colour. It makes a thick, non-invasive clump of narrow spiky leaves 18 inches high with flowering plumes of 3 feet. Old leaves from this are easily tidied away to clean it up in the spring, others such as the pampas grass can be extremely dangerous to deal with except when wearing gloves.

Uniola latifolia is one of the best shortish ones, standing nicely erect and neat with flat green leaves and fine loose panicles of flowers. It keeps compact, looking best standing above lower plants.

Bowles's Golden Grass (*Milium effusum* 'Aureum') is one of the finest for keeping its colour right through the year, attaining a deep golden-yellow in the early spring. Its loose spreading 5–6 inch high clump of leaves are very colourful at the edge of borders and also form a remarkable contrast when planted in clumps around the purple-leaved rhus (*Cotinus coggygria* 'Atropurpurea').

Two taller grasses which are impressive are *Miscanthus sinensis* 'Variegatus' and *M. s.* 'Zebrinus'. Like the pampas grass, these rank as specimens or accent plants in landscape work. In the late spring they start to send up bamboo-like shoots from the base, gradually unfolding a series of long weeping leaves from the growing stem which rises to 4 feet. In 'Zebrinus' the wide leaves are banded crossways with yellow, and 'Variegatus' is very strikingly striped with white.

Molinia coerulea is our own local grass of the Ashdown Forest, a tough, peat-forming grass hard to dislodge in the garden, but it has its attraction when its panicles of dull violet flowers appear in August. More garden worthy is its variegated form *M. c.* 'Variegata', with slender tapering leaves, white striped, forming a thick, ground-covering clump 12–15 inches high.

Holcus mollis 'Variegatus', a dwarf grass, gives a light touch with silvery variegation and is useful for paving or front of the border, but it can be invasive.

The festucas are valuable for rock garden and odd pockets. Apart from *F. viridis* (bright green), they make low, neat silvery-blue tufts that look especially delightful when the early morning sun lights upon them. For those who cannot resist the fascination of seed raising, the half-hardy maize, *Zea mays japonica*, gives a spectacular plant for floral decoration. It needs to be sown early to reach its full maturity—4 feet of very striking silvered variegation along the broad leaves. As with the ordinary maize, this should not be planted out till May. There are many more of these grasses to be sought, so interesting that if room could be spared, a bed entirely of them would be a colourful as well as an unusual feature.

✤ 8 ✤

Carpeters, Ground-cover and Weed Suppressors

THOUGH THE doctrine of ground-covering and carpeting between shrubs and trees may have been a little overdone, it must be admitted that the greater the number of carpeting plants used, the less space there will be for weeds. While in the vegetable garden one cannot practise this, nice clean tidy rows are always good to see, but it means lots of attention with the hoe to get rid of weeds, or hoeing on sunny days before they come. Unless one is fond of extra work, hoeing between shrubs is often impracticable and can do damage to surface roots. The only thing to do with spare spaces in the borders is to play it nature's way and have an effectual cover of plants instead of weeds.

Down in the woods one also finds nature's other cover, a depth of leaves—in matured woodlands, leaf-soil sometimes feet deep, no weeds, but cool and moist below. In and around shrubs this natural mulching is also most effective in arresting any germination of weeds, as well as conserving moisture and providing humus. A deep mulch is also a good deterrent to creeping weeds —smothered and with the light excluded from them, they give up the ghost. So this carpet of leaves is perfectly natural, but ground-covering with a variety of plants is infinitely more beautiful.

The use of perennial creeping plants and others also helps to conserve moisture in the soil as well as providing a tapestry of living greenery of varied beauty, instead of bare spaces. An established heather bed is a fair example of an impenetrable mat of greenery which excludes weeds, saves labour and gives months of colour in due season.

For the foreground of shrub borders, bays between plants and spaces where a shrub needs to be isolated to show its beauty, there are innumerable plants for underplanting that will please the eye, create interest all the year and give colour and contrast during the flowering season. Some of these may be vigorous growers which will often serve their purpose until more compact plants can be substituted. Where there is room enough, these hearty growers are most acceptable, for their prodigality is a boon in time and labour saving. In the end, the compact and slow growers are the ideal to aim at, for they need less curbing and attention, paying their rent in even more carefree ways. Many of the plants described in Chapter 4, The Evergreen Woodlanders and Chapter 5, Other Plants for Shade and Part Shade, come within this category, the evergreens being particularly valuable in giving an air of permanence to the winter furnishing.

Gardening is a most pleasurable occupation dealing with the materials of nature in an attempt to blend them to our will. It is a health-giving hobby which can give immeasurable satisfaction in the results that are achieved, but we never pretend that it cannot be done without some toil. Sometimes it is labour to save labour, but be that as it may, a ground-covering project, though it may take time, will be worth while in the end.

Since *Polygonum affine* was one of our earliest acquisitions and is still with us, it is a fitting one to start with. It is most useful on account of its long flowering period from mid-summer to October and is at its best to the fore of moist borders. Not only does it form a close green mat to the exclusion of weeds but its long, narrow leaves form a carpet of rusty brown and red in autumn and remain so for the winter months. The later summer shows it at its best, with 6-inch long spikes of flesh-pink flowers held erect on 12-inch stems. These charming little heads are wonderful for mixing in little bunches of flowers. *P. affine* 'Darjeeling Red' has 9-inch spikes of crimson flowers which go considerably deeper with age. *P. affine* 'Donald Lowndes' is worth referring to again, as it is such a perfect little ground-coverer for the immediate foreground. It has such quality in its 4-inch, dense, stumpy spikes of warm rose-pink and the leaves also turn a warm rusty tone in late autumn. So much slower growing than the preceding, it is really first-class.

There is no more willing grower among the knotweeds than *P. vacciniifolium*. At times one might mutter about its resolute desire to get the job done and needing some timely snubbing, but each autumn it is realized more and more what a grand plant it is. Its wide, trailing masses produce rosy-pink spikes with the prodigality of heathers. Appropriately, its flowers come with the blue drifts of the autumn gentians, but it must be watched if it is grown with them, for it will encroach to their detriment in no time. It will stand some shade, but never flowers with such abandon there as in a sunny place.

A strong grower in a daintier way is *Veronica peduncularis* 'Nyman's', which gradually creeps into a solid mass of green, rooting as it goes. The impenetrable green carpet looks as healthy in winter time, and all through the summer it sends up hosts of dainty, pale blue, speedwell-like flowers. It will do so in sun or part shade, and is an excellent labour saver.

The epimediums might have been put into Other Plants for Shade and Part Shade (Chapter 5), for that is what they like, and it is there that we use them primarily for ground-cover. Nevertheless, they will grow almost anywhere as long as it is not too dry. Once the exquisite beauty and form of their flowers is fully appreciated they will be wanted in positions where they can be savoured to the full. The dainty composition of the flowers of columbines is easily admired, but with the epimediums one must be more elfin, and then one sees a columbine on a much smaller scale with flower sprays in the 6–12 inch range. You may or may not be intrigued with their little cups and spurs, but you might be determined to get all the sorts you can at all costs!

As ground-covering plants their dense foliage and creeping roots help to make a few more care-free places, and they are particularly effective grouped under deciduous shrubs. Their handsome, low growing and sizeable foliage is no small part of their usefulness, some remaining entirely evergreen and others vying with the best of autumn colours. As the old leaves do not die away before the flowers appear, they are best cut away in early spring when most other border chores are done. A further joy comes after the flowers are over, for then there is the miracle of the gradual unfolding of the lovely fresh green leaves.

For foliage alone, the large-leaved *Epimedium perralderianum* is always outstanding and distinct, and with us remains evergreen. The flowers are yellow and brown. Bold leaved and as strong growing as the last, is *E. pinnatum* with large, rich yellow flowers. Another one with yellow flowers is *E. versicolor* 'Sulphureum' and *E. grandiflorum* (syn. *E. macranthum*) has creamy-yellow ones. The pure white *E. youngianum* 'Niveum' is a species from Japan, one of the daintiest, and worth growing on its own with smaller treasures. *E. alpinum* 'Rubrum' is a small compact grower that goes well with the latter, and has showy dark red flowers. It is a charming family and is by no means lacking in colour and beauty; one of the loveliest, *E.* 'Rose Queen', has quite large flowers of clear rose on 12-inch stems, and then there is *E. warleyense*, which sends up flights of orange and red flowers well above the foliage. These are but a few of these useful woodlanders.

The graceful little *Vancouveria hexandra*, from North America, is also very closely allied to the epimediums and does the same job in as charming a manner. It soon drapes shady places with little fans of soft green, 6-sided leaflets. In May and June it sends up airy 12-inch sprays of delicate little, creamy-white flowers which peep above the leaves.

One of the most useful plants for ground work or for contrasting at the base of shrubs or roses is *Alchemilla mollis*. The size and form of its leaves, kidney-shaped, wavy-edged and soft grey-green, have an especial beauty, perfected to a picture of delight when rain and dew drops gather on them. The 12-inch sprays of small yellowish-green flowers may only appeal to those who like green flowers, but theirs is of such daintiness that in no way are the leaves hidden. It is easily pleased in any soil and makes hearty clumps and gives plenty of children. Another 'ladies' mantle' we have from our old cottage garden is *A. vulgaris*, not to be despised for its name, perhaps a 'cloth cap' in comparison to *mollis*, but an excellent carpeter with its own beauty of leaf and trick of collecting dew and water. *A. alpina* is smaller still in all its ways, but none the less robust. Though its flowers are of no value, its beautiful silvered foliage and desirable compactness always find it a place in the rock garden or odd fill-up places to the fore of the border.

Two late summer flowering plants which are useful as fill-ups and compact cover are *Aster divaricatus* (syn. *A. corymbosus*) and *Serratula shawii*. The aster is an old-time garden plant, an uncommon North American species that has become scarce since the breeding of so many colourful sorts. Yet it has all the good points in its favour for easy gardening, in sun or part-shade it flowers just as well, mixes with all comers and is easily grown. It grows to 18 inches, with fine wiry black stems, very resilient, wind and weather resistant and not needing staking. Individually the flowers are small but produced in close panicles, and the overall effect is a mist of white. It is useful in association with earlier flowering plants such as bergenias or at the foot of the winter flowering hamamelis.

Serrutula shawii cheers the very late days of October to November with soft mauve, cornflower-like blossoms on 9-inch stems. Not in any way a riot of colour but it plays its part, a part that is never any trouble, for it hardly minds where it lives, just a glimpse of the sun will do, and here it forms a close, tufty, frontliner in places where weeds might have been.

In contrast to the last two, once above ground in spring, the dicentras are conspicuous both for a long season of bloom and for their handsome, fern-like foliage. Seeing that they cover quite a bit of ground, we appreciate them more than we used to, and being dwarf they are ideal in the foreground. *Dicentra eximia* and its pure white form bloom for months on end. The rosy-purple heart-shaped flowers dangle gracefully from arching 12-inch stems. Both of these are of very easy cultivation in sun or part-shade, their light airy growth doing no harm when grown close to other plants. *D. formosa* is also beautiful in leaf, less finely cut, but the flowers have a little more red in them. The newer American cultivar *D. formosa* 'Bountiful' is a first-class border plant as well as being good for ground covering. A good clump may soon be obtained by dividing in early spring. The rosy-red flowers are slightly larger and are borne continuously from May till September.

Also for shade and for moist ground is *Houttuynia cordata* from Japan, an uncommon 8–10-inch carpeter. It is a strong grower which creeps along by underground stolons to form an impenetrable thicket of heart-shaped leaves. The foliage is dark bluish-green, interesting and attractive, and a perfect foil to the curious, pure white bracts surrounding the cone of the flowers which peep up through the leaves in the late summer. The rarer double flowered form, *H. c.* 'Flore Plena' also has an appealing charm but ramps in no less a way. Forewarned is forearmed, both will suppress weeds and, likewise, smaller plants. They associate well with the more robust plants of the wild garden—the irises, ferns and hostas.

In the woodland and part shady places *Maianthemum bifolium*, a rare native plant, performs a miracle of dainty carpeting. In a coat of shining green, its broad, grooved leaves have a well bred look, a joy to gaze upon, restful and satisfying in a large carpet. In our peaty soil it spreads far and wide, but so low that all else stands above it. In April to May, erect 3–4-inch stems of flowers arise from between the twin leaves, the daintiest of pure white lily-of-the-valley flowers. It is perfect for carpeting around rhododendrons and other shrubs. In some soils this might not spread so fast and it could be contained in shady parts of the rock garden.

Comparable in its ability to clothe the ground under trees, among shrubs or for the shady side of the rock garden, is *Cornus canadensis* from North American woodlands. It is also a creeper, putting forth large whorls of green leaves from each closely packed shoot. In June this pygmy dogwood puts forth short-stemmed, white flowers with 4 petal-like bracts. Though we have this irresistible little plant at its jolliest of moods, we have never yet seen the red berries which it is said to have, but its final gesture to the ending year is a full redness of the leaf.

In spite of all this ground-cover talk, the lilies-of-the-valley might murmur, 'there is nothing to it, we have done this thing for hundreds of years'. Yes! and how they do do it, only couch grass or ground elder could creep in to mar their beauty of leaf. Yet this grandest of all carpeters can be contrary if the soil is not to its liking. Generally it likes its semi-shade, its soil deep and rich, then if this be its sanctuary, leave it alone to reward you a thousandfold in its beauty and sweet fragrance outdoors or for indoors. The old and trusty favourite is *Convallaria majalis*; then there is the rarer double form, and the not unattractive *C. m.* 'Rosea', a little more than pink, but which for us would not creep into the 'desert island Dozen'. If you like your flowers large, *C. m.* 'Fortin's Giant' may please. For the collector, there is the variegated form striped with yellow on the leaves, but we have not found its variegation constant.

If you want ground-cover with joy and colour, the violas have it all the time, but to be your pride, a little weeding and grooming may be the price to pay. The grooming comes in spring when they should be tidied up and all old growth cut back. Violas may sound a little like bedding out, but they are excellent for the rock garden, edgings, in colonies for ground work and very easily stepped over when taller plants are to be reached. Most of the viola species and garden hybrids are satisfactory to grow, and are happy almost anywhere as long as the soil is reasonably moist and not too arid.

One of our very early favourites was the Grecian *Viola gracilis* which we used to find made foot-wide carpets of purple-violet, seemingly an endless patch of colour. It is difficult to get the true species now, but robust growing hybrid forms are obtainable, including *V. gracilis* 'Aurea' with large sulphur-yellow flowers. *V. cornuta* from the Pyrenees, the horned viola, with blossoms of an elongated shape, is one of the most useful and easy going, maintaining a long succession of lovely mauve flowers. The snow-white *V. cornuta* 'Alba' is one we would always have in the garden. It is no less hearty and beautiful, breeding true from its offspring. *V. cornuta* has given rise to such good garden hybrids as 'Jersey Gem', 'Golden Wave', 'Moonlight' and others of the utmost value.

Some interesting and engaging violet species come from the woodlands of North America, among them *V. cucullata* and *V. septentrionalis* 'Alba'. These lose their leaves in winter time, only nobbly crowns remaining from which the new leaves appear in spring. *V. cucullata*, known as the hooded violet, flowers in May and June; its flowers are quite large, but would be even more endearing if they were scented. The pure white flowers of *V. cucullata* 'Alba' with delicate purple veinings, always look perfect against its bright green leaves and it is lovely grown together with the type plant. *V. septentrionalis* also has very large white violets very generously produced in the summer time. Both of these like a little shade in the south of England. However much these may brighten and cheer the summer months, there is nothing so encouraging and refreshing to the spirit as the wild violets that brave the early days of March. Carpeting round fringes of woodland, there is little to complete with the fragrance of *V. odorata* and the many named cultivars in all endearing shades.

Like the violas, the geraniums provide a round of pleasure in the way of colour as well as furnishing a good amount of greenery to smother the germination of weeds. With their permanence, easy cultivation and total lack of any need of periodic division, they win hands down as one of the best species for the spare-time gardener. Though mentioned in Chapter 3, A Few Front-Line Perennials, *Geranium grandiflorum* 'Alpinum' covers such a space and flowers so freely that it is worth a re-cap. This also applies to *G. macrorrhizum* which not only looks after itself, but is so worth its place for its aromatic, evergreen foliage. *G. ibericum* does its part with solid clumps of greenery which is by no means out of place to the fore and around almost any of the roses. Its great show is in June, when it bears masses of saucer-shaped, violet-purple flowers well above the foliage. Though it will grow and flower in some shade, the colouring of its flowers seems to need sunshine to be seen at its best.

In passing we must mention our native *G. pratense* for its softer shades, pale blue and lavender-blue which make it a perfect combination with roses. Although 2½–3 feet is on the tall side as ground-cover, grown in this way we are spared any staking, for when wind-blown they lean upon the roses and scarcely do any harm. Some say its self-sown seedlings can be tiresome, but in our semi-wildness these fit in, and a mulch of bracken is a moderator to much germination. Another native, *G. phaeum*, the mourning widow, we cherish not only for old times' sake and its coverage, but for a beautiful rosette of leaves. This dusky cranesbill will have a charm for those who like the curious and quaint. Its flowers are dusky-black to chocolate-brown, perhaps not to all tastes, but they have a graceful poise on their 2-foot stems. It seeds about mildly, and it is fun gathering the seeded plants together to widen a planting. *G. endressii* and any of its pleasing children of garden origin can be added to these to be sure of getting a mass of long-lasting colour in various shades of pink.

Quite distinct from all these is *G. atlanticum* from the Atlas

Mountains. It is quite hardy and sends up nodding, 12-inch high deep purple flowers as early as May, but soon goes to ground again. Making a creeping clump, it sends up its fresh leaves in the late autumn. It is little known despite having been in gardens for a long time. Another deciduous and unusual one for geranium enthusiasts is *G. tuberosum* from Europe. It grows from tubers and sends up its finely-cut, ferny foliage in spring. It is more free flowering than *atlanticum*, and foot-high stems bear rosy-purple flowers in June. Both of these are useful medium space-fillers for warm positions, but as they die away after flowering, a good memory for their positions will save them being accidentally dug up. It also applies to *G. grevilleanum* which does not come to life until late spring. It is a newcomer to us and we easily fell for its charms which are freely given in the late summer. The flowers are a lovely old-rose, silvery-pink, large, enlivened with dark anthers and trailing out on long stems. As yet, its semi-trailing habit keeps to a moderate 12–15 inch spread; sunshine seems to suit it.

Two more which can be classed as trailing ground-coverers to spread over a good space are *G. wallichianum* 'Buxton's Blue' and *G. candidum*. 'Buxton's Blue' is fairly well known, but could still be more extensively used, for it has a very long season of bloom, starting to flower about the end of July and going on into the late autumn months unless checked by frost. With cup-shaped flowers of a good violet-blue, an inch across, these are all the more attractive for a white central zone. The flowers hover nicely over the fresh green foliage and later in the season take on a more intense blue. It wisely goes to rest for the winter months, making a welcome reappearance again in late March. During the season its trailing growths will cover a good 2 feet of ground. It is easy and long-lived, but one of the few geraniums that seems to prefer part shade. *G. candidum* from China only arrived between the First and Second World War and so far has not yet been awarded all the prominence that it might have had. It is of much the same habit as the former, a sprawling trailer of great beauty. Starting in late July, the large, shapely, fully-cupped flowers are pure white, attractively adorned with dark stamens—very lovely among the beauty of its scented foliage. With as long a flowering period as 'Buxton's Blue', the flowers have a tendency to nod, so that they are not seen at their best unless grown at the top of a wall or grown so that the sprawling growths will lean or climb against a bush or conifer. While strong and robust, it does not cover quite as much ground as 'Buxton's Blue'. It is best in full sunshine, even in rather poor soil, so that its flower stems are kept shorter and the blooms seen to best advantage.

The native geranium, *G. robertianum* (Herb Robert), has its place in the wilder parts of the garden, but one of the dearest treasures is a small white one. Our reward for rescuing this from a hedge-row which was being bulldozed has been tenfold in numbers and pleasure. Yet so dimunutive is it in comparison to herb Robert, that beyond *G. robertianum* 'Album' we know not what to call it. It spreads in ferny colonies of fresh greenery and gives a delightful multitude of small white flowers right through the season.

One of our most important ground-fillers for growing right up to the grass verges and even helping to deter the edges from growing are the irises. Not the well-known flag irises of such gay display in their weeks of May and June, these are not for our acid soil, but numerous species and forms which have reached this country from the western and eastern States of America, China, Japan and Europe. Unlike the rhizomatous iris (*I. germanica*), these are fibrous and wiry rooted, generally requiring more moisture than the former. They are good perennials for the front of the border, and bays between shrubs generally provide conditions to their liking. They can also be very effectively used in mixed borders, the evergreen ones helping to give some semblance of life in winter.

Of these irises, and one of our standbys—and also one of the longest cultivated in this country—is *I. douglasiana* from America. With a generous mass of thick, shiny, leathery leaves to display for winter effect, some of the older leaves also give a rusty-red to add to its attraction. Good growth and freedom of flower are one of its joys, the blossoms over 3 inches across, sit up well above the leaves on 12–15-inch stems in May. The type plant usually bears flowers of soft blue, but there is no lack of variety, for lavenders, deeper blues and buff shades are all in cultivation.

Iris setosa from North America is another easy tempered one that can be depended upon to fill a good space and appear year after year. For those who admire the beautiful and large flowered, moisture-loving *I. kaempferi*, *I. setosa* has a similarity in size and in the form of its flower, consisting of three large petals, though rounded in the falls and very solid in texture. It is delicately pencilled and veined in gold, altogether a unique iris. The flowers vary through pale lavender and lavender-blue to deeper blues. Its foliage is attractive in itself, broad, a fresh green and gives a fine display in the autumn when it fades away to a brilliant yellow. Although the flower stems stand at over 2 feet, it is one of those plants that can be used in a telling way in the immediate foreground.

Most appropriate for the front row too, is the choice *I. innominata* which forms low mats of evergreen, grassy leaves, indeed the semi-prostrate habit of the foliage gives full view to the lovely flowers. Mostly these blossoms are held on short 6–9-inch stems, and give a wide range of shades from deep blue to lavender and pure yellows, all being some 3 inches across, beautifully pencilled with darker veinings. As they are quite slow growing, individual plants taking some time to cover a foot of space, they are best in groups, and a mixture of forms blend together delightfully; the blue forms are the stronger growers. Also among these smaller irises from the States is the dainty *I. tenax* which sends its blooms up above a mass of grassy evergreen foliage. It is also variable in its colour range with shades of lilac and purple to cream and white. May to June is the flowering time of both of these. They enjoy a soil well enriched with humus and are more impatient of drought than others, and in the south of England succeed in positions away from the fullest sunshine.

In the days of collecting in China, many garden-worthy irises were sent back, a very beautiful one being *I. chrysographes* and its very attractive form *I. chrysographes* 'Rubella'. *I. chrysographes* builds up a clump of neat grass-like foliage which can cover quite an area, then the numerous flower spikes stand up boldly to over 18 inches. It is very free flowering with dark, rich, velvety-purple flowers, very strikingly veined with gold and white markings. It may be used in any moist border or damp margins in open woodland. The latter is always admired, but the form collected by Kingdon Ward, *I. chrysographes* 'Rubella', never fails to get exclamations of excitement for its dark wine-red flowers. Often listed alongside these two is the hybrid *I. chrysographes* 'Margot Holmes' with sumptuous blooms of rosy-purple and inheriting the golden veining and grassy foliage of its parent. Very pleasing, too, is *I. forrestii* from Yunnan, also with quite short, very fine grassy leaves. It flowers in May, bearing clear golden-yellow blossoms veined with purple, and this only rises to 12–15 inches. It requires a fairly moist position or one in half-shade where it may be uniformly moist.

The real moisture-loving irises do their bit of ground-covering and work saving as a foil to the ground-hugging leaves of the primulas and take their place where the ground is lower and with a higher water table. All the same, *I. sibirica* which usually goes with the moisture lovers, is so good tempered and prolific, that as long as the soil is fairly rich and moist it is happy anywhere. Wherever there are stands of *sibirica*, any weeds are effectively stifled by its close grassy clumps. With its long slender stems it is dainty in almost any form, but cultivars such as 'Perry's Blue' sky blue, 'Snow Queen' white, 'Gatineau' azure blue, 'Tropic Night' very dark violet, are great improvements on the type plant; they vary in height from 2–3 feet.

Iris kaempferi does not cover the ground in quite the same way, its broad leaves being more erect, and groups are more effective, but in the quality of its flowers it is a feast for those who love the exotic. The flowers are superb and glorified in comparison to any others, most of them a good 6 inches across, velvety and silky in texture, like great clematis flowers and in many shades. The Japanese endow them with delightfully fascinating names, interpretations of their beauty and merits, such as, 'Morning Mists', 'Purple East', 'Dancing Girl', 'Moonlight Waves' and a host of descriptive poetic rhapsodies. Primarily they are moisture and sun-lovers and are best where they are not too wet in winter time. Generally they are quite happy in a good rich soil if it is well manured in spring and plenty of moisture is given in the growing season. Another species which inhabits marshy ground in China is *I. delavayi*, one of the tallest of these moisture lovers. From long narrow leaves, in June it sends up an imposing stem of 4–5 feet with large, brilliant rich violet flowers blotched with white on the falls.

Iris innominata aurea

Donald F. Merrett

Geranium grevilleanum

J. R. A. Davies

Maianthemum bifiorum growing out of an old pine stump

H. E. Bawden

Campanula jenkinsae

Gentiana × macaulayi

J. R. A. Davies

J. R. A. Davies

Gentiana pneumonanthe. Our native gentian of moist heathlands

Donald F. Merrett

Zigadenus elegans

Gentiana makinoi

Delphinium brunonianum. A satisfactory and rewarding dwarf delphinium

Polemonium pauciflorum

Two lesser irises which are carpeters and both closely related are *I. ruthenica* and *I. graminea*, both forming low grassy clumps suitable for edging. We have had *ruthenica* for many years, flowering freely in some gardens, generally more freely when well established in warm and fairly moist soil. Some people say that it does not flower for them, but it is possible that there are more free flowering forms. It is worth trying in a number of places, for its 4–5-inch stems bear handsome flowers of deep blue, beautifully pencilled with white markings on the falls, and they are produced in May. *I. ruthenica* 'Dykes' is dwarfer and very free flowering, usually performing again in the autumn. *I. graminea* is strong growing, a good fill-up plant for a sunny position. Its flowers are mainly violet-blue, but touches of reddish-blue and yellow add to its attraction. Though borne on rather short stems of only 4–5 inches and tucked away among the leaves, it is free flowering and the flowers have a delicious scent when picked and bought indoors.

An iris which came to us as 'Constantinople Blue' and is still offered under this name, is another fine addition to the front-line fill-ups. It flowers in June when most of the dwarf irises are over and it has flowers very much like *I. reticulata* in form, but of a lavender-blue. It forms a thick grassy clump and is very prolific with its blooms.

As regards covering ground, one of the most useful of the anemone family is *A. sylvestris*, a woodland plant of Austria and Germany. Though this enjoys cool conditions, a moderate amount of sun keeps it happy and more free flowering. It colonizes itself among shrubby plants where it threads a compact way with low ground leafage, handsome, dark and shining. Lilies seem to thrive under its cover, possibly it helps to keep them drier in winter time. The flowers are very beautiful, and Reginald Farrer does it full justice in referring to it as the 'snowdrop anemone', with its luxuriant spectacle of loveliness and certainly a jewel, also likening it to a smaller, rather refined *A. japonica*. It is in April or early May that its big fat buds on sturdy 10-inch stems open to give solid, pure, creamy-white flowers, slightly larger than a ten-penny piece, which have a slight fragrance. When happy it really 'goes to town' and should not be near smaller plants. The most free flowering form is *A. sylvestris* 'Spring Beauty'.

An admirable and pleasing plant is our own native ajuga which peeps up through grassy woodlands in June, giving its mist of blue bugles. The species and cultivated varieties are by no means to be despised as robust evergreens for weed suppressing and for providing a canopy of colourful leaves. With dark, bronzy leaves and deep violet spikes, *A. reptans* 'Atro purpurea' can be a telling foil to carpet under light foliaged shrubs. *A. reptans* 'Variegata' with silver variegation and pale blue flowers is another effective spreader. One of the best is *A. genevensis* 'Brockbankii', a nice stay-at-home plant with 6-inch bugles of soft gentian blue, and for the collector and lover of curiosities, there is *A. pyramidalis* 'Crispa', listed in catalogues as *A. metallica* 'Crispa', with quaintly crinkled leaves and a compact habit.

The special attraction of *Teucrium scordium* 'Crispum' is in its aromatic sage green, extra crinkled leaves, but its flowers are yellowish-green, the same as the wood sage. It started in the rock garden, but proved too robust, but if a garden be big enough, there is usually a place for misfits. Finally, it found a home in the sun in the front of a border, proving its worth by draping a good square foot of ground in a dry problem corner. It is indestructible and beyond cutting off its dead flower spikes in the spring, it requires nothing in the way of cultivation. Furthermore it assists in holding moisture in the soil for its near and more colourful neighbour, *Dimorphotheca barberiae*. Seedlings of it should be discarded as they do not come true.

Some big shrubs and the larger rhododendrons have to be widely spaced, and the ground can be covered with leaves or bracken, but a most natural looking plant for this purpose is *Trachystemon orientalis* (*Nordmannia cordifolia*). Its great, dark green, heart-shaped leaves are very ornamental and much in keeping with the larger shrubs. In spring 18-inch spikes of blue borage-like flowers appear and then the leaves soon start to expand. As long as the soil is not too root ridden, it is one of those very useful plants that will grow in part shade among trees, where it will push up strongly through any mulch.

For the front of any very sunny border, *Cerastostigma plumbaginoides* can be another remedy for weed suppressing. In most districts it is herbaceous, coming to life in the spring with a mass of low leafy growths. When happy it thrusts out in all directions from a close growth of underground stems. It gives a lovely display for weeks in the early autumn, when its 8–9-inch shoots break out with bright blue, phlox-like flowers of half an inch in size. At the same time its foliage begins to take on attractive tones of bright red before it passes away in late autumn.

Sometimes at the end of a border, where there may be a shady end, or near trees where it is dry, one is faced with the problem of covering the ground, but what will thrive? It is the evergreen *Pachysandra terminalis* which will do a sterling job in these circumstances and form a close evergreen cover with its thick glossy leaves. More conspicuous is the form *P. terminalis* 'Variegata' with its leaves creamy-white at the edges. Both of these also serve well at the base of larger shrubs or conifers.

In a poor light soil and warm places, the wonderful emerald green of the camomile, *Anthemis nobilis*, is both restful to the eye and delightful to the senses when its wonderful fragrance is released upon the air. It was much used in Elizabethan gardens as a low plant and for edging. In the modern garden its low spreading habit fits it for paving and spare sunny places where it can be walked upon to bring forth its pleasant scent. There are single and double varieties, the latter being more showy, with its pure white pom-poms. The green clover-like foliage of the blue pea, *Parochetus communis*, is equally restful and lovable. It comes to life in late spring and sets about making its close ground-covering carpet for the summer, spreading rapidly and rooting as it goes, often covering yards by the autumn. Then and far into the winter, if frost does not spoil it, it carries an unending succession of intense gentian-blue, pea flowers which hover above the pretty clover-like leaves. It prefers cool sheltered corners or damp paving pockets. If pieces are put in a pan in early autumn, it can be a delight right through the winter under glass.

One of the humbler little colonizers which helps to smother weeds and is in a natural setting around trees is the little native woodruff, *Asperula odorata*. Its rich green will thread a thick carpet across the ground, yet so light and dainty that it never harms other plants. In May it is a pretty sight when smothered with small pure white, fragrant starry flowers; it must have shade.

✱ 9 ✱

Odds and Ends, and Gentians

THIS CHAPTER was born from the somewhat dry remark of a photographic friend. After taking several pictures and finding it difficult to get a foothold on solid earth, he ventured that we did not waste much space! Indeed, we like it so, for nature herself clothes her ground so well, leaving little room for the hot sun to dry out the soil. To be interesting, a garden should be well filled with a variety of plants, thus, it looks more natural and less prefabricated. Our overcrowding is also due to a love of plants, being collectors of them and coupled with a desire to find the right position or association to make them happy. Even some of the native plants that we are fond of are not all easy to grow, needing just the right environment, and present a challenge to grow them well.

Quite a number of these 'odds and ends' are valuable old plants that perhaps get pushed into the background to make way for newcomers. Some are easy-going old alpine friends which will drape the odd corner or even the ordinary border if it is well-drained. A few of the bulbous plants do not quite fit into the chapters which we have tried to classify others under, but there is always the spare place and often just the right home.

If we take *Patrinia triloba* (syn. *P. palmata*), it is one of a thousand and one non-invasive plants that can be recommended to fit into the small garden. It is known as the yellow valerian, and one that we should especially choose for it is by way of being a slow-growing carpeter, taking quite a few years to cover a mere foot. It does not demand the best of positions, just odd fill-up places where it is cool or even part-shady. Here it will play its quiet part, late in the summer but with quite showy, short-stemmed heads of golden-yellow flowers over prostrate, shining, wavy-edged leaves.

Then there is one of our autumn treasures, *Chrysanthemum* 'Mei-Kyo', which is an absolutely hardy one. This is invaluable in very late autumn for mixing with little posies of gentians, heathers, sprigs of pernettya berries and other oddments. It is only an 18 -incher, sending up a thicket of stems which erupt into hundreds of glowing rosy-pink, inch-wide pom-poms in late September. At the foot of a wall, alongside a medley of earlier flowerers, it gives a last dash of interest right into November.

For springtime there is *Hacquetia epipactis*, which is also *Dondia epipactis*, a name which leaves a loophole for easier remembrance! This might be considered a collector's piece, more for the show-case than the shop-window. Nevertheless, it has quaint beauty, and at a time when one is searching round the garden for some enlightenment any time between February and April. It is a little, green flowered treasure of 4 inches, the flowers consisting of petal-like green bracts which surround a centre of pale yellow stamens, and these are nicely backed by dark green shiny leaves. It is a fascinating, slow growing and compact little gem for intimate shady places, where it will give annual and everlasting pleasure.

Among our collected miscellany, we have an affection for one begonia which is reasonably hardy in a warm sheltered garden, and that is *Begonia evansiana*, a Japanese species. It has been outside for a number of years and while it cannot compare with any of the bedding species for colour, it produces a shower of single pink flowers on 18-inch stems in summer time, and then its large, yellowish-green, red-backed leaves are handsome as well. It does not mind a certain amount of shade and increases itself freely by means of bulbils.

Most of the polygonums are pretty rampant growers and very useful in certain places in the garden. The darling *P. capitatum* is no exception in this way, but unfortunately it is one of the least hardy. However, it makes up for its only shortcoming by seeding itself or being amenable to having rooted pieces potted up for housing under glass. At times it may come through the winter, on the other hand it grows very quickly from spring sown seed. Its flowering capacity is incredible, sending up dense little pale pink globose heads of flower from June right into November. Reddish-brown markings on the leaves add to its attraction and in one summer it will branch and spread over 1½–2 feet of space. It is well placed at the base of any conifers, taller plants, rock garden or paving.

Three other small treasures which give delight are *Calceolaria mexicana, Sedum cepaea* and *Polemonium pauciflorum*. Once you have had the cheerful *Calceolaria mexicana* flowering for you it will perpetuate itself for all time. It is no nuisance, but a charming annual species of 10–12 inches. In sunny places where more robust types of rock garden plants are grown, its pale yellow pouches light up odd places and around other plants. Odd plants of it always give interest and informality among greenhouse pot plants. *Sedum cepaea* forms a low-growing compact rosette of fleshy dark green leaves, looking for all the world like an unusual Kabschia saxifrage. In the summer it throws up sprays of 6 inches which are covered with small pale pink flowers, the general effect being of a baby Japanese cherry. It sows itself anywhere for your everlasting enjoyment, sometimes making a dome of 4–6 inches across before it is ready to flower. *Polemonium pauciflorum* also is not long lived, but children you will have that form orderly little rosettes of finely divided foliage, silvery-grey, and some 3–4 inches across. From these there will be 18-inch spikes of drooping, tubular yellow flowers in June or July. It is an interesting and unusual plant among this genus, its seed is very viable for we have known it turn up years after we have had a flowering plant die.

Aristolochia sempervirens is one of those extraordinary oddities that we always like to grow. It comes from Crete and is worth its place as an evergreen and for its strangely shaped flowers, besides being completely hardy. It forms a mass of creeping, prostrate twining stems well clothed with shining green leaves, the whole giving a closely set bush of 5–6 inches high which will cover a good 2 feet of space. The curiously fascinatingly shaped flowers are produced in the spring, 'Dutchmen's pipes' of purplish-maroon with a yellow throat, which peep out from among the leaves. It likes a warm position, does well in poor soil and may be effectively placed in paving stones or will scramble through dwarf shrubs.

A love of plants often leads to a greater appreciation of the merits of many of our British natives and an urge to grow a few of them. The wall pennywort, *Cotyledon umbilicus* (syn. *Umbilicus pendulinus*), is one which always appeals to our taste for the interesting and unusual, and is a plant which will happily fill a spare shady crevice. It belongs to the crassula family and has evergreen, fleshy rounded leaves of dark green. While it could not be called showy, its curious spike of yellowish-green bells certainly have a charm. It has an ancient air about it, a wildling with no man-made look, a little aloof from the moderns. With a setting in nature of shady mossy ledges, its place is not in the formal garden but somewhere in the cool where it will seed about mildly. A cotyledon of more hearty growth is *C. simplicifolia* (now *Chiastophyllum oppositifolium*), usefully mat-forming with fleshy evergreen leaves. In June this also sends up graceful arching stems, from which dangle a myriad of small yellow flowers. This is for the rock garden or front of the border, for in sun or part shade it is no trouble. Our native saxifrage, *Saxifraga granulata*, is as happy in the garden as it is in any of its meadows. In the garden it is best confined to the wild or where its bulbils will not be forked over and scattered about. Even so, its solid little clumps are never amiss at the edge of the rose beds where its refined, pure white cups tell that the roses will not be long behind. Its double form, *S. granulata* 'Plena', with many petalled little white 'bachelor's buttons' is precious and takes a place in a cool rock garden pocket.

Many years ago we had *Centaurium scilloides* (syn. *Erythraea diffusa*) in the rock garden, a little evergreen carpeter that gave us a cheerful splash of pink in the later months of summer. Now it is here and there and far beyond, little pads of 6-inch wide, pale greenery, even by some chance down in the lower borders 50 yards away. Yet this little treasure, native to Pembrokeshire and Europe, is no nuisance but one of the joys of July. It belongs to the gentian family and when in flower its many short-stemmed heads of bright rose-pink almost hide its tuft of greenery and resemble those of a small flowered, pink *Gentiana verna*. We are also fortunate enough to have the common centaury, *C. erythraea*, as one of our wildings, happening here and there in the various borders, its basal leaves looking like a rosette of *Gentiana acaulis*. This is 6–8 inches and gives an erect umbel of pretty, pale pink flowers from June onwards—a minor joy of nature's legacies.

Geranium dalmaticum is one of those rock garden plants that gives a first-class performance in any well-drained, sunny garden. Its neat cushion forming habit is without comparison among the hardy geraniums, forming so well-bred and close a tuffet that it can rub shoulders with the best at the front of a midget border. Its foliage of light shining green colours well in red and orange before it dies down for the winter. The rounded clear pink flowers match perfectly and have a rare satiny quality, standing erect at 6 inches. The white cultivar is also very desirable. For these a spread of 2 feet may be expected, excellent in a warm paving pocket but where feet may not mar their beauty. Alongside these *Geranium* 'Ballerina' might well be grown, a lusty child from the two alpine geraniums, *cinereum* and *subcaulescens*. This inherits the beautiful silvery leaves of *cinereum* and has 2-inch-wide, flat open pink blossoms, delicately pencilled in a deeper colour. Aptly spraying her blossoms around her, but never completely hiding her lovely corsage, Ballerina flowers almost non-stop till autumn and also proves a good doer.

Two everyday rock garden plants which we always remain faithful to are *Chrysogonum virginianum* and *Horminum pyrenaicum*, both with merit but neither by any means rare or with any particular beauty. Theirs is perhaps a sentimental value, for they were among our earlier choosing. They got hounded from place to place when newcomers arrive, yet they still survive. *Chrysogonum virginianum* is no alpine snob and will do a turn in the front of the border to make a wad of low green foliage and countless 6-inch sprays of bright golden, 5-petalled daisies all the summer through. Unkind things have been said about *Horminum pyrenaicum*: 'it apes the ramondas, tries to be like a dingy salvia in flower and has masses of vulgar leafage'! Yet there it is, we keep it. To say its 12-inch spikes have deep blue, salvia-like flowers might sound flattering; its evergreen leaves always hold some interest, at least more than bare soil! Pink flowered and white forms have their attraction.

Teucrium pyrenaicum is yet another of our early rock garden acquisitions which really is worth its place on account of its rounded hairy, velvety-green foliage all neatly laid out upon the ground and spreading far and wide. Its short woolly heads of little hooded cream and lilac flowers are quaint and will delight those who can descend from worldliness to fairy status. It thrives in sunny places or warm paving pockets. Such a position will also suit *Triptilion spinosum* which we had at one time. This may still be in the hands of a few, and although we cannot trace it again, it is worth seeking as a charming herbaceous plant in the 12–15 inch range. It was collected in the Andes and was quite hardy, only needing an occasional division to keep it in good heart. One of its assets for the rock garden or border of choice plants was its late flowering from June into July, and that desirable quality of a brilliance of blue flowers which came in clusters.

Though essentially a rock garden plant on account of its low growing habit, the so-called blue buttercup, *Anemone obtusiloba* 'Patula', grows quite successfully to the fore of a moist sunny border. It was brought to this country from the mountains of Burma and, like many plants from there, has proved quite hardy, a great merit especially when a plant has beauty and is long-lived as well. Its flowers are a really good blue, widely open, with a striking boss of golden stamens. They begin in April, each bloom lasting a long time, and it continues on and off for months. Its only method of increase seems to be from seed which must be sown immediately it is ripe, and then, with luck, they will germinate the following spring.

Another one of the 'curiously attractive' in our collection of oddments is *Zigadenus elegans*, a bulbous liliaceous plant from North America. This satisfies a personal taste for the unusual and is one that easily fits into those spare shady nooks, or just a cool place. In late spring, its tuft of narrow grass-like foliage appears, and by July the flower stems will have risen to almost 2 feet to bear sprays of greenish-white, ½-inch wide starry flowers with a notable deeper green in the centre. It would appear to be an ideal plant to decorate the pool side. Quite different, but also of the lily family, is *Bulbinella hookeri* (sym. *Chrysobactron hookeri*) from New Zealand. Bulbinellas are a small genus which are only native to New Zealand and South Africa, but *B. hookeri* is the only one which is generally cultivated. It is well worth its place among a collection of unusual plants, for it is easily grown and quite hardy. In late spring its fleshy leaves start into growth to form a basal tuft from which in mid-summer it sends up strong 12–15-inch stems which bear spikes of golden-yellow stars in a dense head much like an asphodel or a dwarf kniphofia. In New Zealand where it is known as the Maori onion, it is a common plant of hill and stream sides, inhabiting damp peaty soils, something which we are able to give it, but it does just as well in ordinary well-drained soil.

In a search for beauty one can hardly go wrong in selecting any of these plants of the lily family, the North American camassias being so accommodating that they will thrive for you in almost any place, moist woodland, near the waterside, naturalized in grass, or in the type of border which holds plants of special interest. These are bulbous plants which flower in May, their slender spikes of blossoms ranging from 2–3 feet in height. At one time the bulbs of *Camassia esculenta* used to be roasted and eaten by the Indians, and it was then known as Quamash. As with the others, this comes to life in the early spring, forming a rosette of narrow leaves from which arise strong stalks of 2 feet or more which will bear the star-shaped, dark blue flowers with golden anthers.

Camassia leichtlinii varies from deep blue to pale lavender, always a striking plant when carrying splendid, robust 3-foot spikes with many wide open flowers over a period of several weeks; the white form, too, is particularly fine. *C. cusickii* has not come our way, but its description of broad yucca-like foliage is a change, and it should have tall elegant spikes of pale lavender flowers. These are reasonable to buy and are most effective in the mass, and it helps that they are easily raised from seed.

Though this book was not meant to cover any great range of bulbous plants, for any type of garden the snowflakes fit in for their ease of cultivation and spring and summer flowering. These are cousins of the snowdrops, good stay-at-home plants, hardy, and multiply into large clumps whether in sun or part shade. The earliest to flower, and so welcome in very early spring, is *Leucojum vernum*, often out by February. Strong 6-inch stems bear tubby white bells, drooping and nodding, each petal with its own magical greenish spot. The variety *L. vernum carpathicum* is most beautiful, its large cups being tipped with a spot of gold, but it is not often offered. There is no beginning or end to the garden year, for these will be spearing the ground well before Christmas. The summer snowflake, *L. aestivum*, is smaller flowered but makes up with a very long succession of snow-white bells swinging from 18-inch stems over a clump of daffodil-like leafage. The Gravetye variety of this has extra large bells. *L. autumnale* is the fairy of the family with enchanting, dangling, pink-flushed tubular bells during September. Like many of the plants of the Mediterranean areas, it thrives in warm sandy soil.

Ornamental garlics may make the uninitiated shudder, but there is much decorative value for the arranger of garden plants in this family of alliums. To this can be added great variety in height, pretty things of a few inches to giants of 3–4 feet, those with wide, interesting globular heads, other dainty treasures with nodding bells of red, white or blue. True to their kind, they will exude a smell, but there is no need to be unkind and tread on them. One usually expects members of the *Liliaceae* to be sweetly perfumed. However, the alliums are not the only rebels in the family for even *Lilium pyrenaicum* is repugnant to some. A tendency of the alliums to scatter their young by free seeding is a fault that leads to caution and a need to put certain of them in the wilder parts of the garden.

Allium triquetrum is one of these, yet never a nuisance, and we cannot deny it a welcome among the low border plants for its 15-inch spikes of white bells. Neither do we despise the old-timer, *A. moly*, another short one; its umbels of bright yellow flowers of June days are as welcome as its compact patch of upstanding, bluish tulip-like foliage. This can be placed to some effect and though it increases fast, at least we have not known it seed. *A. albopilosum* is a different character, handsome in its great flowering umbel, some 10–12 inches in diameter, each flower lilac and star-shaped radiating from an 18-inch stem. Another one with large globular heads is *A. karataviense* with misty pink flowers. This is worth growing for its astonishing broad flat leaves, a very metallic greyish-blue, and most ornamental in the border foreground.

Silvery-green leaves are also the background for the 6-inch, pink umbels of *A. ostrowskianum*. *A. siculum*, a May to June flowerer, has always been accorded admiration, for it stands up strongly at 2 feet with an umbel of gracefully nodding bells of a creamy-yellow, also variable to reddish shades. Flowering bulbs may rest and gradually build up again, but once its seedlings are established there is a succession for flowering. One of the most colourful and reliable is *A. pedemontanum* (syn. *A. narcissiflorum*) about 6 inches high with clusters of nodding reddish bells. Good, blue flowered, small ones are *A. cyaneum* and *A. azureum*, with compact and grassy foliage. All these and a host more for the choosing, are easily cultivated in any average soil and sunny places.

The symphyandras are a different story, more for those who know the joy of giving life and raising plants from seed. They are relations of the campanulas, and while some of them are not very long lived or die when they flower, the garden is considerably beautified with their mass of drooping bells in the late summer. They are easily raised from seed and it is very satisfying to see youngsters steadily building up rosettes of leaves as the time approaches for their flowering. Usually these are plants for the rock garden, specimens that stand up in proud isolation to show off their fountains of loveliness, but as long as a border is sunny, well drained and light-soiled, it is suitable. *Symphyandra wanneri* was our first dip into these, and we were captivated by its long violet bells, nodding from sprays off the main 9–10-inch stem; this is monocarpic. *S. hofmannii* is taller and forms an architectural pyramid of 1½–2 feet, sometimes taking two years to build up its hairy-leaved rosette. It then pushes up to flower with a multitude of almost Canterbury-bell sized creamy bells; this seeds itself freely. There are others to be explored in this beautiful family.

The popular muscaris or grape hyacinths form one of the easiest and free flowering of the spring bulbs, needing little description, but one which satisfies a departure from the ordinary is *M. comosum* 'Monstrosum' sometimes known as the feather hyacinth. Flowering from April to May, it bears wide rounded heads of sterile mauvish-blue flowers on 8-inch stems, giving a misty feathery effect. Like all the others it is easily grown and will endure hot dry positions. It is easily obtained from bulb specialists, not a rarity, but distinct and well worth growing. While it may not be spectacular it will always find a place in the gardens of those who love the curious and unusual plant.

Not many of the numerous ornithogalums are cultivated and even the commoner *O. nutans* and *O. umbellatum* are not seen very much, except in older gardens and collections. We think *O. nutans* is one of the most beautiful, especially for those who are attracted by green in flowers. But this is a subtle combination of muted green and silvery-white together. In April when one is eagerly looking round at all returning life, *nutans* will be showing quite large, drooping campanulate bells, a head of 10–12 silvery-white flowers which are streaked with green on the outside. It has an arresting and distinctive charm, especially against a darker background. More dwarf in statue, *O. umbellatum* (Star of Bethlehem) is particularly useful for edging and massing. It increases rapidly into compact clumps which give a fine display of short-stemmed, starry white flowers in April.

The few dracocephalums that we grow take their place in the rock garden where they earn their keep by late flowering. They are of herbaceous nature, not appearing above ground until the early days of May. The most valuable of these labiates is *Dracocephalum hemsleyanum* which has sapphire-blue flowers, a desirable colour at any time, and in June to July and later, most acceptable. The blossoms are penstemon-like, on flopping 12–15-inch growths. This might be tried in a warm border, though the best we have seen was growing out of a hot wall. If you like dark violet-blue, the 18-inch *D. ruyschianum* is a handsome species and will please you if it has a setting of silvery foliage behind it.

In the early months of the year it is always stimulating to watch the progress that plants have already made towards completing their annual cycle. It is reassuring to see shoots of crocus and irises pushing away at ground level, then at the earliest there is *Sisyrinchium filifolium* spearing the ground and getting ready for its flowering in April. This is a beautiful member of the *Iridaceae* from the Falkland Islands. It is referred to by Reginald Farrer in his book *The English Rock Garden* as the Fair Maid of the Falklands, and his classic description: 'hangs out wide diaphanous bells of a white so delicate that they seem fairy cups of blown glass, freaked and lined with dark threads', is most fitting and real. These are borne on 6-inch stems over a clump of rush-like leaves yet, dainty and frail as it may look, it is a sound perennial, not flinching from the hail and storm that may accompany its first flowers. It will often go on for many weeks and be blooming in early June, almost a month after its beautiful North American cousin, *S. douglasii* (syn. *S. grandiflorum*), has gone to rest. The latter is often in bloom by February or March, outstanding among our early treasures. The nodding silken bells of imperial violet always fire enthusiasm in those who have not seen it before. A not too sunbaked position in the rock garden suits them—with a label to mark their place, for after June they will be resting.

Much later, and in the lovely days of late May, comes *Arenaria montana*, one of the first dozen alpine plants that we ventured upon. Wonderful days of early enthusiasms, and we still grow it now, for it is first-class. It can be too rampant among the choice plants of the rock garden, but in a mixed garden its uses can be manifold. In sunny places even as ground-cover cascading down a slope or over a rock, hanging down from a wall or threading its way through dwarf shrubs, it is superb. The profusion of its shilling-sized snowy-white flowers is amazing.

Two other easy alpines which were early on our list are *Aster farreri* and *A. forrestii*, lovely dwarfs which do well in ordinary, sharply drained soil. *A. farreri*, named after its collector and introduced from Tibet, is a plant for the large rock garden or sunny border. It spreads by offsets and underground runners but never so vigorously as to be a menace. It is easy to fall in love with this aster, for the 12-inch stems stand straight up from the mat of basal leaves, showing beautiful flower heads with large narrow-rayed asters of lavender. The thin rays of the flowers droop from a golden centre, giving a fascinating shaggy appearance; it flowers in late July. *A. forrestii* is also very endearing with large deep lilac-blue, orange-centred flowers on 6-inch stems.

Such sunny positions as these asters enjoy, should also make *Bulbocodium vernum* happy—this is a near relation of the crocus and colchicum. It is offered in bulb catalogues and should be planted as soon as possible in the autumn for it is one of the earliest of the spring flowers to bloom, often being out with the snowdrops.

When in flower it is more like a colchicum but has attractive reddish-purple flowers and the leaves appear at the same time. It multiplies rapidly in good soil and should be divided when the bulbs get too crowded.

In the main the campanula family is very much relished by at least one of the gardener's enemies, the slug. However, it is well worth noting that there are some that escape these ravages, among them being *Campanula sarmatica*, *C. garganica hirsuta* and *C. jenkinsae*, which seem to be disdained, *sarmatica* possibly because the leaves are covered with minute hairs. *Garganica hirsuta* is also hairy, and maybe they do not find it easy going on this type of leaf. As regards *C. jenkinsae*, we do not know the parentage, but it would appear to be in form and habit near to our own *C. rotundifolia*, which is also left well alone. *Sarmatica* from the Caucasus is tough and hardy, and is also one of the earliest of this family to flower, usually in late May or early June. It is a vigorous plant, clump forming though by no means invasive, and one plant will only occupy a space of 6–8 inches. It is suitable for the rock garden or border and stands more sunshine than many others. Its flowers are semi-pendant bells on 12-inch stems and an unusual delicate grey-blue, large and widely open, covered with minute hairs and bearded within. *Jenkinsae* is a very fine white campanula, an older hybrid which is not often seen these days. The large bells are freely borne on erect 10-inch stems, larger than those of *rotundifolia*, but much the same shape. It is a good and permanent doer, standing a good deal of neglect and not asking for the frequent division and attention that some require.

The third of this useful late flowering family is *C. garganica hirsuta*. There is a fascination about the way the trailing flowering growths spray out from the central clump and cling to a rock face or wall. The effect of the grey woolly-leaved foliage and masses of misty, starry-blue flowers is quite something to look forward to on a well-established plant. This is one of the easy campanulas; June is its flowering time, after which—having performed its seed function—the growths die back, leaving a central rosette of evergreen leaves for the winter. The cultivar *C. garganica* 'W. H. Paine' also appears to be slug proof and is a plant of real value for the rock garden. It forms a close 10–12 inch clump which remains evergreen. The star-shaped lavender-blue, white-centred flowers sit close on the mat of foliage.

Wallflowers are among the most valuable of our spring flowers and are favourites with most gardeners, not only for their choice velvety colours but for their delicious scent. Indeed, they have been favourites for centuries and it is fortunate that while many flowers have been improved and lost their scent, wallflowers seem to be unaffected by this reforming. Of the choice old garden kinds and doubles, the old Scots wallflower, *Cheiranthus* 'Harpur Crewe' is the best and most enduring in a poor soil where it will make a sturdy bush of 18 inches high; on a richer diet a severe winter may account for it. Its chief flowering time is during May and June when it sends up spikes of very fragrant, small, rich golden buttons in clusters, but it will also brighten most months of the year with odd blossoms. While many people grow these old favourites, there are also the species and their hybrids which give good spring colour and an equally pleasant scent; in catalogues these will be found under *Cheiranthus* and *Erysimum*. These are mostly low growing, carpeting and cushion forming in habit but, like the larger bedding plants, will grow and endure in any poor soil, and are best suited for sheltered borders, walls and slopes away from cutting winds.

One of our favourites is *C. mutabilis*, a most attractive beauty, dark foliaged, low growing and of bushy habit, averaging 5–6 inches in height. Its flowers have all the soft velvety attraction of the taller varieties, but undergo a remarkable change as the spring days go by, transforming from soft purple to subtler shades of soft lilac and even to bronze and buff as they age and pass away during its many weeks of flowering. *Mutabilis* will spread into a bosky, shrubby clump and cover some 18 inches of ground. It will flower at intervals during the summer and again in the autumn when its colour is more beautiful and intense. We have had plants last as long as six to seven years and even when severe weather may cripple some growths, they will break away happily from the base in later spring. A very lovely hybrid is *C.* ×. 'Moonlight', very well named, for its yellow flowers have that soft luminous quality of full moonlight. It is of the same bushy habit as the former but not so wide spreading and only 4–5 inches high. *C.* 'Newark Park' is another little favourite of low, bushy, ground-covering habit with bronzy-orange flowers. E. K. Elmshirst with dark green foliage and more erect habit is almost non-stop with its rich purple flowers so that it is always difficult to get cuttings from it.

Among the smaller species, generally included in *Erysimum* are *E. rupestre* (syn. *E. pulchellum*) and *E. pumilum* which, for their small tufted habit, are most suitable for the rock garden. *E. pumilum* is a choice little plant which forms domes and green tuffets of narrow foliage, and in March and April will produce large heads of a good yellow which will soon hide the evergreen hump. *Rupestre* also makes a close mound with masses of brilliant gold blossoms in early spring. *E. linifolium* is another first rate little plant of bushy habit, low growing, sometimes almost prostrate and giving pale lilac-purple flowers in the spring and later in the summer. It is not a very good perennial, but obliges by sowing itself into stony crevices. One which we have been delighted with is *E. concinnum* from California which, after four years, has so far proved quite hardy. Attractively grey-leaved, it is low spreading and compact with large rounded heads of a lovely pale cream. It is sweetly scented and blooms in the spring.

One of the delights of having a rock garden or small border is a more intimate approach to these dwarf plants which may be overlooked in a larger border. The dwarf delphinium species are all the better for the sharper drainage of the rock garden and they are interesting and unusual, as well as providing bright colours. One which is both uncommon and curious and survives year after year is *D. brunonianum* from the high Alps of Tibet. This is only 10–12 inches high and has curious rounded, hairy flowers of pale violet-blue in July. Another small species which has brilliant peacock-blue flowers is the earlier flowering *D. grandiflorum* (syn. *D. chinense*). *Tatsienense* is similar with long spurred blossoms of azure blue. Both of these are not very long lived, but flower very quickly from seed. One usually assumes that these delphinium species will be blue, but the Californian *D. nudicaule* flourishes a sparkle of quaintly shaped scarlet and yellow flowers, a brilliant show as a group with the sun upon them. This species is perennial in a warm raised position, though a few years seems to be its limit. It is perfectly hardy but the fleshy tuber-like roots do not go very deep and are apt to be lifted by hard frosts, and must be pushed back again before they dry up. The flowers come in July, carrying up to a dozen or more flowers on a 12-inch stem and side branches.

In addition to the blues of these alien delphiniums, our native *Lithospermum purpureo-coeruleum* and *Echium vulgare* (viper's bugloss) can be useful and handsome plants for the wilder parts of the garden. Those who have chalky soil and cannot grow the wonderful *Lithospermum prostratum* in any form, can comfort themselves with *L. purpureo-coeruleum*, which has really large, deep blue flowers. It is not a plant to put near small treasures, for it sends out long sprays which bend to the ground to form new plants, but it can be accommodated as ground-cover on sloping banks. On the other hand, it can be very effective as a single plant by cutting the runners off.

Most lovers of wild plants know *Echium vulgare*, its mists of blue covering the chalky Down and waysides. Since we introduced it into the garden, not a season passes without some self-sown seedling raising up 3-foot spires with innumerable, almost gentian-blue flowers all the way up, and from the leaf axils lower down. Incidentally, one of its most admired efforts was self-sown into a convenient paving crevice, but sad to say its honour was diminished, almost denounced when named as a native plant! It is rarely a perennial. For those who find room for a few annuals, *E.* 'Blue Bedder' can specially be recommended as a very compact, dwarf cultivar with an exceptionally long flowering period and with deep, bright blue flowers.

In pathways and paving where room may be found for it, the creeping evergreen *Pratia angulata* from New Zealand can be most rewarding. Keeping absolutely prostrate, it rapidly threads its way across the soil, rooting as it goes. All through the summer and through the autumn it is set with small, starry, lobelia-like white flowers which are followed by a generous crop of large, astonishing purple berries. This is most showy in a moist paving pocket and will even do well running along at the grass verge, quite happily threading its way into it and flowering in the grass. More New Zealanders which are ideal for gritty or sandy pockets are the raoulias. Our own revel at the sides of a gravel path and form tight mats of fascinating greenery. The minute *Raoulia australis* flows down the path in glistening silver, and in later summer erupts into a thousand baby flowers of golden-yellow. *R. glabra* advances in a solidified carpet of emerald green, upon which sits a host of stemless white flowers, singularly large in comparison to the misty effect of *australis*. A little loose in growth but in silvery-green, *tenuicaulis* binds down another sandy path. This is studded with small yellow flowers.

While speaking of gravel paths, whereas weeds will seed into them, so also will it yield a bonus of all manner of self-sown treasures for the garden and distribution to friends. The path, the happy home of the raoulias, only consists of 6 inches of surplus sandy gravel which had to be disposed of, yet it is astounding how well certain alpines prosper in it. No doubt it would be too spartan for some, but the tuffets of the saxatile *Erinus alpinus* could scarcely be more at home than in their alpine haunts and have naturalized themselves for all time, and give a rosy-purple edging to the path. It does much to prove that eternal cultivation hint of 'well-drained' has some foundation! This erinus might be too disorderly for some, but their operation to smother weeds is worth while. Here, too, the silvery pattern of *Antennaria dioica* creeps more closely than in rich soil, and thymes and sedums like the warmth that they get. The greeny film of *Arenaria balearica* enjoys the shady side and climbs up the rock edge. *Mentha requienii*, a microscopic mint, is also among these, a wee film of green upon the surface, but a mighty atom of *crème de menthe* when trodden upon!

We have never delved into the vast sedum family overmuch, but there are many valuable for their foliage, and the fact that they are so easily grown and will exist in the poorest soil. There are many to choose from, but for our own 'desert island choice', it might well be *Sedum populifolium* for its quaintness. It is distinct in its tree-like trunk of some 10–12 inches, and its late summer flowering is an asset. Its leaves are like those of a poplar and the white flowers are hawthorn-scented. *S. kamtschaticum* 'Variegatum' is an attractive low growing one which is handsomely variegated in green and silver and has orange-yellow flowers. Our others might well be *S. spathulifolium* varieties, everybody's plants, but so well worth growing and colourful in their wads of glaucous spoon-shaped leaves which colour so brilliantly in the winter time.

To those who have never seen it before, the mouse's tail, *Arisarum proboscideum*, is always a source of wonder and delight, one of nature's captivating curiosities. Partly hidden among the large spear-shaped leaves, the large flowers (spathes) appear like a crowd of little gnomes in council, but the intriguing part is the long dark maroon tails waving out among the leaves. Its creeping mass of low leafage forms a ground-covering carpet. It is easily grown and prefers some shade; it dies away in the autumn.

Others of these fascinating woodlanders are *Clintonia uniflora*, *Trientalis europaea* and *Polygonatum falcatum*, low growing little treasures for carefully selected places. We are lucky in this respect, as part of our old quarry is walled into rock pockets which provide separate little woodland retreats which give some check to those that need a little discipline. *Clintonia uniflora* is rather scarce in cultivation but it turns up occasionally if close watch is kept upon those exciting annual catalogues from nurserymen. It is one of the engaging plants that haunt the woodland glades of the United States. In late spring it sends up tufts of broad, luxuriant glossy foliage, a telling background for the slender-stemmed pure white starry flowers which are succeeded by blue berries. It spreads happily in any peaty acid soil.

Trientalis europaea is not for any garden show, but it is a rare British native of northern woods, and is a baby plant which is perfect for wandering about cool soil among dwarf shrubs and rhododendrons. It is a frail little thing with a pretty whorl of oval leaves, over which hover dainty, starry, pearl-white flowers. It grows from a very small tuber and is not easy to establish, we were lucky enough to import it in a rhododendron and it has colonized itself.

Polygonatum falcatum is a miniature Solomon's seal from Japan, a dainty little plant of 6–8 inches high. It has slender little rhizomes which spread well in cool shady places. In spring it sends up leafy stems from which hang inch-long Solomon's seal flowers of creamy-white.

Though interest in the garden may wane a little by mid-summer, to us the great thrill of these later months is the glory of the gentians. These are indeed an indispensable family, and very important, since they begin in July, are at their best in August and September and, in mild spells, we have picked blooms of *Gentiana sino-ornata* in December. Nearly all gardeners have seen or are familiar with the wonderful blue of *G. acaulis*, that tantalizing spring flowering beauty that always has us guessing as to whether it will flower or not. In this respect the autumn gentians are free flowering, not only rivalling *acaulis* in their blues, but having a wider colour variation in their shades, ranging from rich deep blue to pale Cambridge blue.

There is no denying the appeal of blue flowers to so many of us, but for really heavenly blues the gentians are supreme. Often, they are regarded as plants for the experts or only for the rock garden, but many of them can be recommended for open situations in borders, or open bays between shrubs. While some are temperamental and not everybody succeeds with them, there are a large number that are easy to grow as long as the soil is uniformly moist. The autumn gentians are all alpine plants, coming from the high mountains and alps of China, the Himalayas and a few from Japan, all growing where there is no lack of a moist atmosphere. Considering this, the majority of them are more obliging in cultivation than some other high alpine plants. Nevertheless, there is no royal road to their cultivation, but they will respond willingly to a good moist, friable, deep, well-drained soil which has been boosted with quantities of leaf-soil or peat. It is important to see that they do not dry out during drought periods and especially when flowers are beginning to form.

In the south of England we find that they do best in positions away from the direct sun, in the sunshine, yet 'with their backs to the sun', that is, the western exposure. With a little ingenuity it is possible to have success with them in any lime-free soil, be it light, heavy or medium in texture. The medium and light soils always need plenty of peat or leaf-soil, or well rotted compost below—the addition of some well-weathered clay can be helpful to give body to very light soil. Heavy clay will often grow gentians to perfection as long as it has almost its own weight in coarse grit and peat well worked into it.

Gentiana farreri is one of the first of the Asiatic species to flower, starting in late July and often continuing into September. It does not mind lime, but will do better in a lime-free soil. In its original form its large, wide open Cambridge blue flowers had an enchanting quality of heavenly brilliance. Yet now, such a precious quality seems missing, it has lost its spiritual feature and become more worldly, but withal splendid and lovely in its best forms. It is always distinguished by its tuft of very grassy foliage. Starting to flower at the same time as *farreri* are two first-class hybrids, *G.* × 'Inverleith' and *G.* × *carolii*. Inverleith was raised at the Royal Botanic Garden, Edinburgh, and was the result of crossing *G. veitchiorum* and *G. farreri*. It is a really good garden plant, strong growing, with the characteristic of long prostrate stems which produce large trumpets of a vivid dark blue for many weeks. *G.* × *carolii*, though smaller flowered than others, is a willing little grower, putting up an incredible number of blossoms from mid-August to the end of September. Said to have *farreri* blood (*farreri* × *lawrencei*), it has captured some of the intensity of *farreri* in its Cambridge blue.

Gentiana × 'Macaulayi', one of the earliest hybrids raised from *sino-ornata* and *farreri*, has wide open flowers of brilliant turquoise blue and shows the influence of *farreri* in the white-throated trumpets. It is not so robust as 'Inverleith', but it is always in flower three to four weeks before *sino-ornata* and continues well into October.

By mid-September the rest of the Asiatic gentians and other hybrids come into the picture with their dazzling blue, open trumpets. *G.* × 'Kingfisher' is one of these, more recent and said to be of the same parentage as *macaulayi*. The darker foliage of *sino-ornata* is evident, also inheriting its vigorous growth, which makes it an easy plant to divide in the spring. It blooms four to five weeks earlier than its parent and is aptly named, for when well established in a close clump, its masses of vivid blue flowers sit short-stemmed and tight upon the grassy mat. *G.* × 'Midnight', another strong grower of *sino-ornata* parentage, blooms four to five weeks earlier than the parent, giving magnificent dark blue flowers.

Gentiana sino-ornata comes in at the 'grand finale', unsurpassed and superb with masses of deep blue trumpets from late September onwards, and well into December if the weather be kind enough. It is a gentian for all who have a lime-free soil and it is a wonderful plant to mass round the front of moist borders; it can also look well in some rose beds. For cold gardens this is sometimes too late for the full opening of its flowers, but there are earlier flowering forms such as *G. sino-ornata* 'Praecox' and *G. sino-ornata* 'Brin Form'. *Praecox* has proved its worth over a long period of years by flowering regularly by 10th–15th August, together with *farreri*. In this earlier season, with more sunshine, one can enjoy a full expanding of the flowers for many weeks. The only difference in the flower is a slight and attractive hint of violet in its blue. 'Brin Form' is distinct and worth having in any collection for its earlier flowering. It differs in its thin, grassy, narrow-leaved foliage and long, spreading, wandering growths, and is a good grower with deep blue flowers, slightly paler than *sino-ornata*. A treasure for the connoisseur is *G. sino-ornata* 'Alba' which we find usually flowers before its blue counterpart. Though by no means so robust, its flowers are a little bit smaller, but a very good white. It is well worth having but we find it needs fairly frequent division to keep it in good heart and we topdress it twice a year with good gritty soil.

Three gentians which come from Japan are *makinoi, jesoana* and *scabra*. *Makinoi* is one of our favourites, and is always admired for its wonderful violet-blue. Though the blossoms do not open fully they are unique for their size and baggy tubular shape. This, combined with its singular colouring, makes it one of the most showy of this type of gentian. It is easy in moist half-shade, sending up erect, dark flowering stems clothed in glaucous-green leaves. Growing up to 1½–2 feet, established plants will send up twelve or more shoots with numerous heads of flowers in the later weeks of August. *Jesoana* is much akin to the latter, also growing up to 2 feet. It also has no basal rosette, the crowns for the following year's flowering being formed in the late autumn; by the New Year they are prominently above ground. After flowering, both of these set seed very quickly and will often disperse it before the last flowers have faded. *G. scabra* is much later flowering and not at its best until late September. The lovely deep blue trumpets are on 12–15-inch stems. It dies down completely soon after flowering and it is not until the middle of April that shoots are visible. It is an easy plant to grow where part shade will give a position retentive of moisture.

Our own dear native *G. pneumonanthe* is worthy of special note as being perfectly easy to grow in any reasonably moist border or pocket of the rock garden. Though known as the marsh or bog gentian, it does not actually grow in marshy ground, but in heathy ground, sometimes close to swampy patches, and in such places often in company with the asphodel. Though we have plants in the garden, it is always an annual pleasure to seek it on its natural heathland and to find it peeping up through the grasses, we always hope to find a white form. With erect trumpets of deep blue, open flowers on wiry, erect, 12-inch stems, it starts to flower at the end of August, with still a few flowers open in late September. Easily raised from seed, it will flower in its second year.

An earlier one to flower, from China, is *G. gracilipes*, for many years in cultivation as *G. purdomii*, still found in catalogues under that name. It is a long-lived garden plant, one of the treasures that we were delighted to see after years of war neglect, still pushing out strong stems and lovely blue flowers from a tangle of weeds. It is usually in flower by late June, sending out trailing stems to 12–15 inches, turning up at the ends to show the flowers as they develop and begin to open. It flowers first from the terminal head, and then progressively down the stems, prolonging its season of bloom well into July. The trumpet is narrow, but opening to half an inch across, a very good deep blue to violet-blue, opening well in dull weather. Though deciduous, it will spring to life again by March, soon showing a promising and satisfying rosette of narrow, dark green leaves from which the flower stems radiate.

Gentiana septemfida, G. lagodechiana and *G. freyniana* are closely related and very similar, and are everybody's gentians that will flourish in any reasonably cool soil. They can always be relied upon to send out thick masses of semi-prostrate growths which end in clusters of sapphire-blue trumpets in July.

No garden should be without the European species, *G. asclepiadea*, the willow gentian, so effective for shady borders, woodland planting, the waterside and between shrubs. It is a gracious plant, sending up masses of arching stems 2–3 feet high, topped with trumpets of violet-blue to azure blue in late July and August. It is a strong grower of easy cultivation, generally naturalizing itself, sometimes producing very lovely white forms.

Even taller, one of the aristocrats, and of great architectural value, is G. *lutea*, the meadow gentian of the mountains of Europe. It is the giant of the genus, a handsome, robust and easily grown plant that does not call for all the care and attention that needs to be bestowed upon its smaller brethren. The beauty of *lutea* is in its large, deeply ribbed leaves, its tall, stout, flowering spike, and the tufts of yellow flowers borne in tiers of four to five. As a bold foliage plant its deeply ribbed leaves can compare with the handsome veratrums of the same mountains. *Lutea* is to be seen at its best in deep rich, moist soil unparched by direct sunshine. Though a group of *lutea* may be grown in a mixed border, it is more effective and arresting as an isolated group or specimen towering and arising from a low planting. Needing no stake for support, the proud erect stem reaches its maximum of 3–4 feet by July. It then starts to flower in clusters of yellow flowers from the axils of the leaves, and lasts well into August before all the tiers are completed. It is not always easy to obtain as seed is the only satisfactory means of increasing it. While by some standards it may be a little slow to reach flowering size, it is with satisfaction that an annual increase in size and foliage can be observed. However, when it has put great deep roots into the ground and gathered strength to flower, an annual performance may be expected.

If you can please even these few gentians, you will be amply rewarded by their glory. Then, no doubt, you will be tempted and will seek among others the lovely spring gentian, G. *verna*, that treasure for the rock garden. Besides these beautiful gentians, it is all these small plants, a thousand and one of them, that help to make an interesting garden. They fit into the small spaces, or an evergreen one may help to cover the bare winter appearance of any deciduous shrub. Besides those included with the 'Odds and Ends', many other plants help to knit into the picture, including good tempered rock garden plants which will grow in any ordinary well-drained soil. 'Well-drained' soil is often repeated, for it is the key to success with the great majority of plants, so few of them will endure permanently wet, boggy soil.

Some of us enjoy gardening for the sake of the relaxation and pleasure of the physical exercise, the mowing of grass, the cleaning and tidying which brings the satisfaction of a task well done. But, sooner or later, the pleasure and enjoyment from flowers may lead you to want to grow more species and different varieties, and then on to more difficult and exotic plants. In all, there is the pride of achievement, and let us face it, modest as most gardeners are, a certain amount of showmanship enters into it.

However, if this leads you to be 'collectors of plants', you will have happy times searching and seeking them out in nurseries and catalogues. You will find that if you are looking for a certain plant, its name, and the place from which you obtained it becomes imprinted on your memory and it is not so easily forgotten. Almost all the plants mentioned here can be obtained from one nursery or another. For some of them, you may have to look through many lists, but for the searching you will find a vast amount of interesting and instructive information in them. Like so many hobbies, sooner or later the 'collecting bug' may take hold— it may take the form of a great interest in certain families of plants, or in unusual ones or curiosities, in plants from certain countries, or merely in the association of plants that blend well together. In general, we think the reason is often a combination of a search for beauty in plants and flowers, and those which are complementary to each other. Yet, as gardens grow smaller, one must in time become critically selective, restraining oneself to certain favourites and the small compact growers which take up less room and will enable us to grow as big a collection as space will permit.

We must confess that for ourselves we are collectors of plants, but it is chiefly for their charm or beauty rather than rarity and a pride of possession. We endeavour to arrange them so that they stand out well or are accentuated by others. Planning their position is a matter of individual taste, observation, and a knowledge of how they grow, combined with a readiness to adventure and move some when necessary. Success in the choice of the right position for some difficult plant can be very satisfying.

We have tried as far as possible to give a portrait of each plant, its flowering time, height, general spread and the sort of conditions that it likes, and we hope that our experiences may be helpful. Enjoy your garden, enjoy your work, and above all, make a habit of pottering and contemplating.

INDEX

Acaena adscendens, 128
  buchananii, 128
  glauca, 128
Acanthus mollis, 109
  'Latifolius', 109
Aceriphyllum rossii, 98
Achillea argentea, 124
  clavenae, 124
  clypeolata, 124
  kellereri, 124
  tomentosa, 127
Acidanthera bicolor 'Murielae', 32, 33
Aconitums, 113
Aconitum 'Bressingham Spire', 114
  lycoctonum, 114
  wilsonii, 114
Actaea spicata, 99
Agapanthus africanus, 22
  campanulatus, 21
  'Headbourne Hybrids', 22
Agrostemma coronaria, 50
Ajuga genevensis 'Brockbankii', 146
  metallica 'Crispa', 146
  reptans 'Atropurpurea', 93, 146
    'Variegata', 146
Alchemilla alpina, 136
  mollis, 115, 136
  vulgaris, 136
Allium albopilosum, 155
  azureum, 156
  cyaneum, 156
  karatavense, 156
  ostrowskianum, 156
  pedemontanum (syn. *A. narcissiflorum*),
    156
  siculum, 156
  triquetrum, 155
Amaryllis belladonna, 23

Amsonia salicifolia, 59
  tabernaemontana, 59
Anaphalis margaritacea, 45, 123
  triplinervis, 45, 68, 123
  yedoensis, 45, 123
Anemone hepatica, 77
  narcissiflora, 40
  obtusiloba 'Patula', 153
  sylvestris 'Spring Beauty', 145
  tetrasepala, 39, 40
Anemonopsis macrophylla, 16, 89
Angelica archangelica, 117
Anomatheca cruenta, 33
Antennaria dio ca, 127, 163
Anthemis cupaniana, 123
  nobilis, 147
Anthericum liliago, 107
  liliastrum, 107
  ramosum, 107
Antirrhinum asarina, 28
  glutinosum 'Roseum', 28
  sempervirens, 29
Arenaria balearica, 163
  montana, 158
Aristolochia sempervirens, 150
Arnebia echioides, 35
Artemisia canescens, 123
  lactiflora, 114
  nutans, 123
  palmeri, 123
  schmidtii 'Nana', 127
  stelleriana, 122
  valesiaca, 123
Arum creticum, 104
Asarina procumbens, 28
Asarum proboscideum, 164
Asperula odorata, 147
Asphodeline lutea, 47

Aster divaricatus (syn. *A. corymbosus*),
   70, 137
  farreri, 158
  forrestii, 158
  thomsonii 'Nana', 61
Astilbes, 107
Astilbe chinensis pumila, 65
  crispa, 65, 66
  'Perkeo', 66
  glaberrima 'Saxatilis', 16, 66
  simplicifolia, 65
Avena sempervirens, 131

Baptisia australis, 43
Begonia evansiana, 149
  'Abendglut', 71
Bergenia ciliata, 71
  afghanica, 71
  cordifolia, 71
  crassifolia, 71
  delavayi, 71
  'Delbees', 71
  'Silberlicht', 71
Blechnum penna marina, 78
  spicant, 82
  tabulare, 82
Borago laxifolia, 59
Bowles' Golden Grass, *see* Milium
Boykinia aconitifolia, 89
Briza maxima, 131
Bulbinella hookeri, 153
Bulbocodium vernum, 158
Buphthalmum salicifolium, 65
  speciosum, 110

Calamintha nepetoides, 68, 121
Calceolaria mexicana, 150
Callirhoe involucrata, 20
Caltha palustris plena, 88
Camassia cusickii, 154
  esculenta, 154
  leichtlinii, 154
Campanula alliariifolia, 43
  carpatica, 64
  garganica 'Hirsuta', 159
  glomerata, 64
  jenkinsae, 159
  lactiflora, 43
    'Pouffe', 64
  latifolia 'Macrantha', 43
  poscharskyana, 64
  rotundifolia, 64, 159
  sarmatica, 159

  trachelium, 43
  'W. H. Paine', 159
Cardamine trifolia, 16, **73**
Carlina acaulis, 31
Catananche caerulea, 27
Celsia cretica, 27
Centaurea gymnocarpa, 18, **125**
  macrocephala, 120
Centaurium erythrea, 151
  scilloides (syn. *Erythrea dffusa*), 151
Ceratostigma plumbaginoides, 146
Ceterach officinarum, 82
Cheiranthus 'E. K. Elmshirst', 161
  'Harpur Crewe', 161
  'Moonlight', 160
  mutabilis, 160
  'Newark Park', 161
Chelone barbata, 34, 52
  obliqua, 52
Chiastophyllum oppositifolium, 151
Chrysanthemum densum amanum (syn. *C.*
  haradjanii), 52
  'Mei-Kyo', 149
  parthenium 'Plenum', 123
Chrysogonum virginianum, 152
Cimicifuga racemosa, 119
  simplex, 119
Cineraria maritime, *see* Senecio
Clematis heracleifolia 'Davidiana', 49
  recta, 49
Clintonia uniflora, 164
Cobaea scandens, 36
Convalleria majalis, 138
  'Fortins Giant', 139
  'Rosea', 138
Convolvulus althaeoides, 23
  mauritanicus, 23
Coreopsis verticillata, 44
Cortaderia selloana (syn. *C. argentea*), 131
Cotinus coggyria 'Atropurpurea', 131
Cotyledon umbilicus (syn. *Umbilicus pendulinus*), 151
Crambe cordifolia, 111
Crinum powellii, 22
  album, 22
Curtonus paniculatus, 110
Cyclamen, 84, 85
Cynoglossum nervosum, 65

Delphinium brunonianum, 161
  grandiflorum (syn. *D. chinense*), 161
  nudicaule, 161
  tatsiense, 161

Dentaria polyphylla, 98
Dianthus, 69
Dicentra eximea, 137
  formosa, 137
  formosa 'Bountiful', 137
  spectabilis, 119
Dierama pulcherrima, 32, 109
Digitalis ambigua, 98
  ferruginea, 98
  purpurea, 97
  mertonensis, 97
Dimorphotheca barberiae, 24, 146
  'Compacta', 24
  ecklonis, 24
  'Prostrata', 24
Diplarrhena moraea, 39, 42, 121
  '*Alpina*', 42
Dipsacus fullonum, 119
Dodecatheons, 106, 107
Doronicum cordatum, 58
Dracocephalum hemsleyanum, 29, 157
  ruschianum, 157

Echinacea purpurea, 47
Echium 'Blue Bedder', 162
  vulgare, 162
Epimediums, 135
Epimedium alpinum 'Rubrum', 136
  macranthum (syn. *E. grandiflorum*), 136
  perralderianum, 136
  pinnatum, 136
  'Rose Queen', 136
  versicolor 'Sulphureum', 136
  warleyense, 136
  youngianum 'Niveum', 136
Erinus alpinus, 163
Eriophyllum lanatum, 123
Eryngiums, 125
Eryngium alpinum, 126
  bourgatii, 126
  giganteum, 126
  oliverianum, 126
Eryngium variifolium, 126
Erysimum concinnum, 161
  linifolium, 161
  pumilum, 161
  rupestre (syn. *E. pulchellum*), 161
Erythroniums, 103
Erythronium californicum, 104
  dens-canis, 104
  grandiflorum, 104
  hendersonii, 104
  revolutum 'Johnsonii', 104

'White Beauty', 104
  tuolumense, 104
Eucomis comosa (syn. *E. punctata*), 38
Euphorbia characias, 115
  cyparissias, 56
  epithymoides, 56
  griffithii, 115, 116
  lathyrus, 114
  mellifera, 115
  myrsinites, 56
  segetalis (syn. *E. portlandica*), 56
  sikkimensis, 116
  wulfenii, 115

Fennel, *see* Ferula
Ferula communis, 118
  'Purpurea', 118
Festucas, 132
Francoa ramosa, 77
  sonchifolia, 77
Fuller's teasel, 119

Galax aphylla, 75
Galtonia candicans, 32, 120
Garrya elliptica, 34
Gaura lindheimeri, 50
Gazanias, 25
Gentiana acaulis (syn. *C. excisa*), 59, 165
  alpina, 60
  asclepiadea, 168
  carolii, 166
  clusii, 60
  farreri, 166
  freyniana, 168
  gracilipes (syn. *G. purdomii*), 168
  'Inverleith', 166
  jesoana, 167
  'Kingfisher', 166
  lagodechiana, 168
  lutea, 169
  'Macaulayi', 166
  makinoi, 167
  'Midnight', 166
  pneumonanthe, 168
  scabra, 167
  septemfida, 168
  sino-ornata, 44, 165, 166
    'Alba', 167
    'Brin Form', 167
    'Praecox', 167
  verna, 169
Geranium aconitifolium, 67
  anemonifolium, 51

Geranium cont.
  atlanticum, 140, 141
  'Ballerina', 152
  candidum, 141
  dalmaticum, 152
    'Album', 152
  endressii, 67, 140
    'A. T. Johnson', 67
    'Rose Claire', 67
Geranium grandiflorum 'Alpinum', 67, 140
  grevilleanum, 141
  ibericum, 140
  lowei, 51
  macrorrhizum, 66, 140
  nodosum, 67
  phaeum, 140
  pratense, 140
  psilostemon (syn. *G. armenum*), 52
  renardii, 66
  robertianum, 142
    'Album', 142
  sanguineum, 66
    'Album', 61
    'Lancastriense', 66
  tuberosum, 141
  wallichianum 'Buxton's Blue', 141
Gladiolus byzantinus, 32
Glaucium flavum, 126

Haberleas, 81
Hacquetia epipactis, 149
Helichrysum angustifolium, 124
  bellidioides, 124
  fontanesii, 124
  petiolatum, 124
  rosmarinifolium 'Purpurascens', 124
  trilineatum (syn. *H. splendidum*), 122, 124
Heliotropium peruvianum, 36
Helleborus argutifolius (syn. *H. lividus* 'Corsicus'), 75
  atrorubens, 75
  foetidus, 75
  kochii, 76
  niger, 74
    'Altifolius', 75
  orientalis, 76
  'Potters Wheel', 75
Helonias bullata, 78
Hemerocallis fulva, 42, 95
  'Kwanso' *flore pleno*, 42
  nana, 42
  thunbergii, 42

Hepaticas, 77
Heracleum mantegazzianum, 110
Heuchera micrantha, 96
  racemosa, 96
Hieraceum bombycinum, 126
Holcus mollis 'Variegatus', 132
Hosta albomarginata alba, 95
  'Aurea maculata' (syn. *H. fortunei aurea*), 94
  crispula, 95
  decorata 'Thomas Hogg', 95
  fortunei, 94
    albopicta, 94
  glauca, 94
  lancifolia, 94
    albomarginata, 94
  plantaginea, 95
  sieboldiana, 94
  tardiflora, 95
  undulata, 94
  ventricosa, 94
Houttuynia cordata, 137
  flore pleno, 138
Hypericum calycinum, 83

Incarvillea 'Bees Pink', 27
  brevipes, 27
  olgae, 27
  variabilis, 27
Inula ensifolia, 68
Iris bucharica, 35
  chrysographes, 143
    'Margot Holmes', 144
    'Rubella', 143
  cristata, 105
    'Alba', 106
  delavayi, 144
  douglasiana, 142
  foetidissima, 80, 129
    'Lutea', 80
    'Variegata', 129
  forrestii, 144
  gracilipes, 16, 105, 106
  graminea, 145
  innominata, 143
  japonica 'Variegata', 130
  kaempferi, 144
  ochroleuca, 113
  pallida 'Variegata', 129
  pseudacorus, 113, 129
    'Variegata', 129
  ruthenica, 145
    'Dykes', 145

Iris cont.
  setosa, 142, 143
  siberica, 144
  'Constantinople Blue', 145
  tectorum, 34, 35
  tenax, 143
  unguicularis (syn. *I. stylosa*), 34, 35
  verna, 105
Isatis tinctoria, 118

Jeffersonia dubia, 103

Kirengeshoma palmata, 97
Kniphofia caulescens, 117
  corallina, 117
  galpinii, 117
  'Maid of Orleans', 117
  'Royal Standard', 117
  rufa, 117

Lamium galeobdolon 'Variegatum', 128
  maculatum, 129
    'Aureum', 31, 129
Lapeyrousia cruenta, 33
Lathyrus aurantiacus, 67
  cyaneus, 67
Lavatera cachmeriana, 111
  olbia 'Rosea', 111
Leonotis leonurus, 37
Leucanthemum hosmariense, 130
Leucojum aestivum, 155
  autumnale, 155
  'Gravetye', 155
  vernum, 154
    carpathicum, 155
Liatris spicata, 44
Libertia formosa, 28
  graminifolia, 28
  ixioides, 28
Ligularia clivorum, 112
  'Desdemona', 112
  veitchianum, 112
  wilsoniana, 111
Linaria dalmatica, 52
Linnaea borealis, 79
  americana, 79
Linum flavum, 68
  monogynum, 38
  narbonense, 38
  perenne, 38
Liriope graminifolia, 54, 55
Lithospermum purpureo-coeruleum, 162
Lobelia cardinalis, 41, 114

Lychnis coronaria, 50
  'Atrosanguinea', 50
  dioica flore pleno, 53
  viscaria, 65
    flore pleno, 65
Lysimachia ciliata, 87
  nummularia 'Aurea', 129
Lythrum salicaria, 46
  'Lady Sackville', 47
  'Robert', 47
  'Rose Queen', 47
  'The Beacon', 47

Macleaya cordata, 117
Maianthemum biflorum, 138
Malvastrum lateritum, 26
Marrubium candidissima, 127
Matteuccia struthiopteris, 120
Meconopsis betonicifolia, 91, 100
  cambrica, 92
  integrifolia, 92
  napaulensis, 92
  quintuplinervia, 92
  villosa, 92
Melittis melissophyllum, 87
Mentha requienii, 163
  rotundifolia 'Variegata', 128
Milium effusum aureum, 131
Mimulus cardinalis, 88
  ringens, 88
Miscanthus sinensis 'Variegatus', 131
  'Zebrinus', 131, 132
Molinia coerulea, 132
  'Variegata', 132
Moraea spathacea, 21
Morina longifolia, 46
Mossy saxifrages,
Muscari comosum 'Monstrosum', 156

Nerine bowdenii, 22
  filifolia, 22
Nierembergia repens, 33

Oenothera acaulis (syn. *O. taraxacifolia*),
  20, 56
  cinaeus, 55
  fruticosa 'Youngii', 55
    'Yellow River', 55
  glaber, 55
  missourensis (syn. *O. macrocarpa*), 20,
    56
  odorata 'Sulphurea', 20
  tetragona 'Riparia', 55

Omphalodes cappadocica, 79
Onopordum acanthus, 119
  arabicum, 119
Ophiopogon japonicus, 55
  spicatus, 54
Orchis maculata, 91
  maderensis, 91
Origanum vulgare 'Aureum', 69
Ornithogalum umbellatum, 157
  nutans, 157
Orobus aurantiacus, 67
  cyaneus, 67
Othonnopsis cheirifolia, 29
Ourisia coccinea (syn. *O. elegans*), 81
  macrophylla, 81

Pachysandra terminalis, 147
  'Variegata', 147
Paeonia cambessedesii, 48
  emodii, 49
  mlokosewitschii, 49
  obovata 'Alba', 48
  officinalis, 49
  veitchii woodwardii, 48
Pampas grass, *see* Cortaderia
Paradisea liliastrum, 107
Parochetus communis, 147
Patrinia triloba, 148
Peltiphyllum peltatum (syn. *Saxifraga peltata*), 110
Penstemon barbatus, 34, 52
  campanulatus 'Evelyn', 34, 121
  'Garnet', 34
  isophyllus, 34
  'Schoenholzeri', 34
Perovskia atriplicifolia, 18, 130
Phalaris arundinacea 'Picta', 131
Phlomis fruticosa, 53, 122
  viscosa, 53
Phlox divaricata, 61
  maculata, 40
  ovata, 61
  'Norah Leigh', 30, 40
  pilosa, 61
  subulata 'Fairy', 61
    'G. F. Wilson', 61
    'Temiscaming', 61
Phormium tenax, 109
Phygelius capensis, 51
  aequalis, 51
Phytolacca americana, 118
Platycodons, 63
Polemonium pauciflorum, 150

Podophyllum emodii, 103
  peltatum, 103
Polygala chamaebuxus, 81
  'Purpurea', 81
Polygonatum falcatum, 164
  multiflorum, 90
  officinale flore pleno, 90
  verticillatum, 90
Polygonum affine, 134
  'Darjeeling Red', 134
  'Donald Lowndes', 59, 134
  amplexicaulis 'Speciosum', 52
  bistortum 'Superbum', 52
  capitatum, 149
  vacciniifolium, 61, 135
Polystichum setigerum, 120
Potentilla alba, 62
  argyrophylla 'Atrosanguinea', 63
  erecta 'Warrensii', 63
  forrestii, 59
  'Gibson's Scarlet', 63
  megalantha, 63
  rupestris, 67, 68
  tridentata, 62
  'Yellow Queen', 63
Pratia angulata, 162
Primula alpicola, 100
  'Violacea', 100
  beesiana, 99
  bulleyana, 99
  chionantha, 101
  denticulata, 99
  florindae, 100
  helodoxa, 79, 99
  'Inshriach Hybrids', 101
  involucrata, 100
  japonica, 99
    'Red Hugh', 99
  pulverulenta, 99
    'Miller's Crimson', 99
  rosea, 100
  secundiflora, 80, 100
  sikkimensis, 100
  vulgaris, 99
  'Wanda', 99
Prunellas, 69
Pulmonaria angustifolia, 87
  'Mawson's Variety', 87
  'Munstead Blue', 87
  officinalis 'Alba', 87
    'Rubra', 87
  saccharata, 87
Pulsatillas, 60, 61

INDEX

Pulsatilla vulgaris, 124

Ramondas, 81
Raoulias, 163
Rehmannia angulata, 33
Reineckia carnea, 78, 85
Rheum palmatum, 112
  kialense, 112
Rogersia aesculifolia, 116
  pinnata, 116
  podophyllum, 116
  tabularis, 116
Rohdea japonica, 85
Rosa 'Little White Pet', 59
Roscoea alpina, 101, 102
  cautleoides, 102
  humeana, 102
  purpurea, 102
  'Procera', 102
Rubus fockeanus, 83
Ruta 'Jackmans Blue', 122, 125

Salvia candelabrum, 30
  chamaedryoides, 31
  fulgens, 31
  glutinosa, 30
  haematodes, 30
  involucrata 'Bethellii', 31
  jurisicii, 31
  pratensis, 30
  tenori, 30
  sclarea turkestanica, 29
Saponaria officinalis flore pleno, 50
Saxifraga cortusifolia, 96
  'Rosea', 96
  cuneifolia, 96
  fortunei, 16, 82, 95
  geum, 96
  granulata, 151
  'Plena', 151
  hypnoides, 96
  mossy varieties, 72
  peltata, *see* Peltiphyllum
  rotundifolia, 96
  sarmentosa, 82
  umbrosa, 71
    'Variegata', 71
    'Melvillei', 71
    primuloides, 71
    'Ingwersens Variety', 71
Schizocodon soldanelloides, 74
  'Magnus', 74
Schizostylis, 26

Scilla peruviana, 37
Scopolia carniolica, 89
  podolica, 89
Scrophularia aquatica 'Variegata', 128
Sedum cauticola, 62
  cepaea, 150
  kamtschaticum 'Variegatum', 163
  maximum 'Atropurpureum', 45
    'Versicolor', 45
  populifolium, 163
  'Ruby Glow', 62
  roseum, 56
  spathulifolium, 163
  spectabile, 44, 61
    'Brilliant', 44
    'Carmen', 44
    'Meteor', 44
  telephium, 45
    'Autumn Joy', 45, 62
    'Munstead Red', 45
    'Roseum Variegatum', 45
Selinum carvifolium, 118
Senecio, *see also* Ligularia
  cineraria, 18, 22
  greyi, 122
  leucostachys, 125
    'White Diamond', 18
Serratula shawii, 137
Shortia galacifolia, 73
  uniflora 'Grandiflora', 74
Sisyrinchium douglasii, 158
  filifolium, 157
  striatum, 121
Smilacina racemosa, 90
  stellata, 90
Sphaeralcea munroana, 26
Spiranthes spiralis, 91
Stachys lanata, 58, 65
  'Olympica', 58
  macrantha, 58
Statice mouretii, 27
Steironema ciliata, *see* Lysimachia, 87
Stokesias, 62
Stylophorum diphyllum, 93
Symphyandra hofmannii, 156
  wanneri, 156
Synthyris reniformis, 80

Tanakaea radicans, 78
Tellima grandiflora, 72
Teucrium orientale, 127
  pyrenaicum, 152
  scordium 'Crispum', 146

Thermopsis montana, 44
Thymus doefleri, 125
  lanuginosa, 125
  mastichina, 125
  nitidus, 125
Tiarella cordifolia, 72, 93
  polyphylla, 72
  trifoliata, 16, 72
Tigridias, 36, 121
Trachystemon orientalis, 146
Tradescantias, 47, 48
Tricyrtis hirta, 90
  latifolia, 89
  macropoda, 89
Trientalis europaea, 164
Trillium grandiflorum, 106
Triptilion spinosum, 153
Trollius europaeus, 108
  ledebouri, 108
  pumilus, 108
  ranunculinus (syn. *T. patulus*), 108
Tropaeolum polyphyllum, 37
  tuberosum, 37

Uniola latifolia, 131
Uvularia grandiflora, 98

Vancouveria hexandra, 136
Veratrum album, 93
  nigrum, 93
Verbascum bombyciferum, 18, 130

  chaixii 'Alba', 112
  named cultivars, 112
  vernale, 112
Verbena bonariensis, 25
  corymbosa, 41
  'Lawrence Johnston', 25
  rigida (syn. *V. venosa*), 25
Veronica cinerea, 65
  crassifolia, 57
  gentianoides, 57
  incana, 58, 127
  pectinata 'Rosea', 127
  peduncularis 'Nyman's', 135
  prostrata (syn. *V. rupestris*), 58
  spicata, 57
    'Barcarolle', 57
    'Blue Peter', 57
  sumilensis, 57
  teucrium 'Trehane', 31, 58
Vincas, 83, 84
Violas, 139, 140

Waldsteinia ternata, 84
Woad, *see* Isatis, 118
Wulfenia amherstiana, 80
  baldaccii, 80
  carinthiaca, 80

Zantedeschia 'Crowborough', 105
Zea mays japonica, 132
Zigadenus elegans, 153